Your Complete Guide to
Making & Decorating Perfect Layer Cakes

ANYONE CAN CAKE

WHITNEY DEPAOLI

CREATOR OF

Sugar & Sparrow

PAGE STREET
PUBLISHING CO.

PAGE STREET
PUBLISHING CO.

First published in 2023 by
Page Street Publishing Co.
27 Congress Street, Suite 1511
Salem, MA 01970
www.pagestreetpublishing.com

Distributed by Macmillan, sales in Canada by The Canadian Manda Group.

27 26 25 24 23   2 3 4 5 6

ISBN-13: 978-1-64567-682-9
ISBN-10: 1-64567-682-X

Library of Congress Control Number: 2022939289

Cover and book design by Josiah DePaoli
Photography by Whitney DePaoli, Josiah DePaoli and Abi Porter

Printed and bound in the United States

For Josiah, my biggest supporter
and co-dreamer.

For Theo, my tiny sous chef.

And for my mother, who started me on this baking journey.
I'll carry your spirit with me forever.

CONTENTS

INTRODUCTION

My kitchen was in chaos. There were cake scraps and buttercream all over the counters and the floor. Dirty dishes blocked the faucet. Ingredients were scattered around and used cake tools were everywhere. Nonetheless, I stood before my very first layer cake in complete awe. I had filled it, stacked it, frosted it with my smoothest layer of buttercream yet, covered it in a layer of pale yellow fondant and finished it all by piping some intricate designs in royal icing. As I look back now, I'm sure it wasn't anything special, but at the time I was completely enamored. It looked just like I had imagined! I marveled at what I'd created with my own two hands.

Beyond satisfied with my creation, I started cleaning up. Smiling wide, I danced around the kitchen, washed the dishes, wiped the counters and tucked all my tools and ingredients away. I was carried by the bliss of my first successful cake, and the kitchen soon looked even cleaner than it had before I started. I took another peek at the cake. Instead of another wave of pride, I felt a pit in my stomach as I saw the ripples forming on the sides. A mysterious bulging ring had formed around the entire cake. All of my ornately piped royal icing was becoming distorted as gravity took hold and my once beautiful cake quickly turned hideous. I stood in my sparkling clean kitchen and burst into tears. After having a good cry about the cake's fate and thanking my lucky stars that no one but I had seen it, I took to the Internet to figure out where I'd gone wrong.

This all happened long before cake decorating tutorials were plentiful on YouTube. My web searching led me to a DVD called *Perfecting the Art of Buttercream* by Sharon Zambito, which promised to help "prevent blow-outs and bulges." Exactly what I needed. I waited for it to arrive in the mail and I popped it into the DVD player as soon as I had it in my hands. Watching it made me realize where I'd gone wrong: I had over-filled my cake layers. I didn't create a sturdy enough structure for the filling. Not only that, my chocolate ganache filling was too thin to uphold the cake layers on its own, which resulted in the dreaded bulge. As soon as the DVD ended, I played it again. I kept watching it on repeat, scribbling down notes as I went.

I tried the cake again with the new techniques I learned. This time, no bulge. No rippled sides. No distorted decorations. I successfully made the cake I'd once imagined, and it inspired me to keep on learning and creating.

Maybe you've been there too. You wanted something more than the average sheet cake, but it didn't quite come together. But you made that cake because you realized something: Creating a beautiful, delicious cake as a labor of love has the power to bring happiness to any occasion. Whatever special event or milestone happens in our lives, cake can help amplify joy.

That's the thing I love most about cake: the pure joy it brings wherever it goes. I've seen that joy in the eyes of brides and grooms, close friends and complete strangers at birthday parties. Almost everyone lights up when they see a cake. When a delicious cake is all wrapped up in a thoughtful design, it becomes something more than the average dessert—it's made much more meaningful through all the planning, the baking, the creative visuals, the mouthwatering anticipation and the memory of enjoying it with people you care about.

Throughout the years, I've interacted with plenty of people who wanted to make a "fancy cake," but they thought it would be too difficult or they simply weren't sure where to start. Through all my cake work, I've been privileged to see many people step out and try their hand at making a cake outside their comfort zone only to totally blow away their family and friends. It's because of moments like those that I love sharing recipes, decorating tutorials and cake-making secrets through my blog, videos, social posts, messages, chats and phone calls. I want to make the world a more joyous place, and it's a thrill to imagine that happening one cake at a time.

So out of all the things to become passionate about, why cake? It all began when I was barely tall enough to look over the countertop, side by side with my mom in the kitchen. I remember flipping through her recipe books and running my fingers over the glossy pictures of rustic layer cakes, hypnotized by the frosting swirls that looked almost too pretty to eat. Not long after, I found myself making the recipes from her books on my own. To tell the truth, it began mostly because I liked to eat the results—but I also found that I was fascinated with the magic of baking. The fact that you could create something delicious just by following some directions and mixing different ingredients together blew my little mind.

Although I was drawn to baking from a young age, it wasn't until I started watching a cake decorating show on TV in my early twenties that I realized how much can be done with cake. Inspired, I headed to my local craft store and bought a simple collection of cake decorating supplies. Shortly after, I faced my cake-bulge disaster before I was saved by Sharon Zambito's *Perfecting the Art of Buttercream*. Once I learned the basics, I scoured YouTube for any decorating tutorials that existed and started making art out of cake layers and frosting. I gave these cakes to my neighbors and offered to make a friend's birthday cake, looking for any excuse to practice techniques. What kept me coming back to the kitchen and the craft store was that moment of pure, unfiltered joy when I handed my creations to their recipients. Even better was when I got to witness them taste the cake, savor a delicious treat and create memories on the spot.

All of these free cakes started turning into requests for weddings and all kinds of celebrations. I slapped together a quick website, certified my home kitchen and printed some business cards. Before I knew it, I was working a full-time day job and coming home to make cakes until the wee hours of the morning. I was both completely exhausted and entirely invigorated.

This kind of work was not without its fair share of cake fails. There was the time I stayed up until three o'clock in the morning making my first tiered wedding cake and, in my tiredness, sat on (and broke!) every single gumpaste flower I had made days before. There was the time I caught my oven on fire trying to make a Butterbeer-flavored cake for a Harry Potter fan. I've dropped cakes, had cakes collapse, overfilled cake pans, watched a cake melt in the sun and tested recipes hundreds of times because they just weren't right.

Through it all, I learned that—even with all my failures—anyone can make a great cake. I wanted to share what I'd learned and hopefully save others some failure, so I started a blog to see who might be interested. For the past few years, I've dedicated my time to crafting recipes and filming detailed cake decorating tutorials. I realized I had come full circle in my cake journey: I was now teaching people of all skill levels to make cake, just like those first recipe books, YouTube videos and cake decorating DVDs had taught me. I created my blog for everyone, because I believe that anyone can make pretty cakes with the right knowledge and tools.

This book has been a wonderful chance to gather up and pass on things that I've learned over the past few decades. I've even thrown in a bunch of new surprises that I learned and invented as I overcame cake fails, which led to more dancing around the kitchen over cake successes. I want to teach you all the basics I've picked up along the way and show you that it's possible to transform your creations into works of art that look as beautiful as they taste. I want to give you trusted, go-to recipes that you can use to bless other people and make your community a more joyous place. Furthermore, this book is meant to live in your kitchen as a resource so you don't have to scour the Internet for info in a panic.

I've made it my life's work to teach others all of this because I know the joy a cake can bring, and I want you to be able to experience that joy firsthand as you create cakes for clients, give cakes to loved ones and even as you simply gaze on—and eat—the fruits of your labor. I truly believe cake makes the world a more beautiful place. So, let's have fun and make some cakes that you're completely enamored with!

Chapter 1
BAKING THE PERFECT LAYERS

Making some of my first cakes, I did a lot of things wrong, even though I didn't realize it at the time. I can vividly recall opening the oven door repeatedly to sneak peeks, measuring the flour incorrectly (yes, there is a right and wrong way!) and adding cold eggs to the batter. It turns out these are all big no-nos in the baking world. Once I learned the reasons why, it changed my baking for the better.

In this chapter, we'll cover all the basics of baking your cakes—from prepping your ingredients to the moment you take your cake out of the oven. These things may seem small, but they can have a huge impact on the success of your cakes. It's worth investing the time to master basics like how to properly measure ingredients, prepare cake pans and work with your unique oven. Whether you're a longtime baker or you have never made a cake before, working on these basics will pay big dividends later on.

TEN TIPS
FOR CAKE BAKING SUCCESS

Baking the perfect cake layers takes more than just finding a great recipe. Since baking is so scientific, the fine details can make or break your results. Here are ten ways you can set yourself up for cake baking success.

1. **Start with room-temperature ingredients.** The words "room temperature" aren't placed next to certain ingredients in a recipe just for fun. Baking is a science, and in order for the right chemical reactions to happen in the cake baking process, it's crucial that you start with room-temperature ingredients where specified. Here's why: When they are at room temperature, the eggs, butter and dairy in a cake recipe form an emulsion that traps air in the batter. Once you place that batter in the oven, the trapped air expands and gives your cake a good rise and a lovely, tender crumb. It'll happen only when you use room-temperature ingredients, so if you want your cake to live up to its true potential, don't skip this step.

2. **Use fresh baking powder and baking soda.** Did you know that baking powder and baking soda both have a 6-month shelf life once you open them? These two ingredients have an extremely important job in your cake recipe: They're responsible for helping your cake rise in the oven. Each of these leavening agents become activated when they come into contact with liquids. If they're expired or not at full potency, the chemical reaction that causes your cake to rise won't happen. This could mean your cake becomes overly dense or sinks in the middle instead of rising. Be sure to write the date on your baking powder and baking soda when you open them, so that you know when to refresh your supply.

3. **Use the paddle attachment on your stand mixer.** There are all sorts of attachments that come with stand mixers, but the best one for mixing cake batter and buttercream is the paddle attachment (also called the flat beater attachment). It's designed to help prevent overaerating your batter in the mixing process. In other words, it won't allow as much air into the batter as other attachments. Having the right amount of trapped air in your cake batter is a good thing, but if there's too much air incorporated, your cake may end up overly dense or it may collapse in the middle. It is still possible to overmix with a paddle attachment, so be sure to follow the recommended mixing times in each recipe's instructions.

4. **Know your substitutions.** There are times when you're looking over an ingredients list and realize you don't have everything. I recommend heading to the store at this point, because I believe that a recipe should be followed precisely the first time around. This way, you know the full potential of the recipe. The second time around, though, feel free to substitute certain ingredients and experiment a bit, but know that there are some things that are critical to the recipe and can't be left out or adjusted. I've provided a list of common substitutions on page 215 to help you swap ingredients with success.

5. **Be careful not to overmix or undermix.** Have you ever seen the phrase "Be careful not to overmix" in a cake recipe and wondered when to stop mixing? Yeah, me too. That's why I always include the mixing times every step of the way. It helps to have a timer handy to follow along with these mixing times, as they've been tested thoroughly to prevent overmixing and undermixing. Overmixing a recipe means adding too much air to the batter, while undermixing means not adding enough air. Both can ruin the structure and texture of your cake.

6. **Use light-colored cake pans.** Since dark-colored pans absorb more heat than light-colored pans, they tend to brown the bottom and edges of your cake more quickly, resulting in overbrowned cake layers. If you want those cake layers to be perfectly baked, use a light-colored pan instead. I recommend anodized aluminum cake pans by Wilton or Fat Daddio's for best results.

7. **Prepare your cake pans.** Nothing ruins a cake project like realizing your cake is stuck to the pan and impossible to release in one piece. To save yourself this stress, be sure to prepare your cake pans before pouring the batter into them. You'll find my recommended method for preparing cake pans on page 21.

8. **Know your oven.** All of my recipes are written with conventional ovens in mind. If you have a different kind of oven, such as fan-assisted, you'll need to slightly alter the oven temperature and baking time to ensure you don't overbake the cake layers. In addition, remember that many ovens have quirks—they can run too hot or too cool or have hot spots. Use an oven thermometer to track your oven's quirks and make adjustments to your baking process. Page 219 explains all of this in detail, so you'll know exactly what to do.

9. **Don't open the oven before it's time.** I know it's so tempting to sneak peeks of your cake while it's baking, but did you know that every time you open the door, it changes the oven's internal environment? Although it seems innocent enough, opening the oven door allows steam and heat to escape, which can easily interrupt your cake in the baking process. This can lead to sunken and unevenly baked cakes as the temperature changes and hot air gets released. Instead, reach for the oven light to check on your cakes until you've reached the minimum time stated in the recipe you're following.

10. **Remove the cakes from the pans to cool.** When you take your baked cakes out of the oven, it's common to walk away and let them cool in the pan. Cake pans retain a lot of heat, though, meaning they can continue cooking your cake as it's cooling. This can cause the cake to shrink away from the sides of the pan and leave you with uneven edges. To prevent this, I like to let the cakes cool in the pan for no more than 5 minutes, after which I carefully release them and place the layers on a cooling rack or baking sheet to let them finish the cooling process. This way, your cake layers will stay nice and uniform with vertically level edges.

YOUR ESSENTIAL
BAKING TOOLS

1. Stand Mixer

2. Cooling Rack

3. Measuring Cups

4. Whisk Attachment

5. Measuring Spoons

6. Parchment Paper

7. Kitchen Scale

8. Paddle Attachment

9. Oven Thermometer

10. Whisks

11. Sifter

12. Cake Pans

13. Silicone Spatulas

14. Mixing Bowls

You'll find a list of my favorite brands for all of these baking tools at sugarandsparrow.com/tools.

HOW TO PROPERLY MEASURE INGREDIENTS

When it comes to baking cakes, being a perfectionist about measuring ingredients can truly pay off. Since baking is so scientific, and science involves precision, the way you measure ingredients can make or break the entire recipe. There are two main methods of measuring ingredients: measuring them with a kitchen scale and measuring them manually. All the recipes in this book will include both weight and manual measurements.

USING A KITCHEN SCALE

Weighing ingredients is the most accurate way to measure them, because there can be so much variation between manual measurements—especially if you're using the wrong method (more on that shortly). Many people have a set of measuring cups, so it can be tempting to see a scale as a needless addition. If you're serious about baking, I highly recommend investing in a digital kitchen scale to ensure your recipes are always precise.

Using a kitchen scale is simple: Place a container on top of the scale, zero out the scale, then add your ingredient to the container. After you add the first ingredient, zero out the scale again and then add the next ingredient. Repeat this process, making sure to zero out the scale between ingredients (see Tip).

TIP:

Zeroing out the scale between ingredients isn't mandatory, but it saves you from having to do the math of adding ingredient weights together as you go along.

MEASURING INGREDIENTS MANUALLY

While weighing ingredients is the most accurate method, it's still possible to achieve precision with measuring cups and spoons. The measuring process will vary depending on the type of ingredient. The following sections will teach you how to measure each one properly.

Flour

This is the most mismeasured ingredient of all, and it's also critical for providing structure in your baked goods. While it may seem to make sense to scoop your measuring cup through the flour bag and level it off from there, the flour can become packed in the cup and you could actually end up with 50 percent more flour. No matter what kind of flour a cake recipe calls for, adding too much will result in a dense crumb. Use too little flour and the cake will collapse.

What about sifted flour? This depends on where the word *sifted* appears in the recipe. If a recipe says, "1 cup (133 g) all-purpose flour, sifted," sift the flour after you've measured 1 cup (133 g). If a recipe says, "1 cup (133 g) sifted all-purpose flour," sift the flour before measuring 1 cup (133 g).

How to Manually Measure Flour

Use a spoon to scoop the flour into your measuring cup until a heap has formed on top, then level it with the back of a butter knife.

Baking Powder & Baking Soda

These leavening agents tend to settle in their containers as they sit on the shelf. Before you measure, give the containers a little shake or stir with a measuring spoon to unsettle the powders.

How to Manually Measure Baking Powder & Baking Soda

Scoop your measuring spoon through the leavening agent until you have a heaping spoonful. Level it off with the back of a butter knife or use the container's built-in leveler.

> **TIP:**
>
> Baking powder and baking soda both expire after 6 months. When you open baking powder and baking soda, write the date on the containers so you can refresh them before they lose potency.

Granulated Sugar

Unlike flour, it's perfectly fine to scoop granulated sugar, since it's much heavier and less likely to become packed down in the measuring cup. Although it's much more forgiving than flour, sugar does more than just sweeten a cake. It's partly responsible for the structure and softness of a cake crumb, so it's important to use the amount a recipe calls for. Don't try to lessen the amount of sugar in hopes that you can make the cake less sweet, especially without first trying the recipe as it's written. Too little sugar could negatively affect the softness and structure of a cake.

How to Manually Measure Granulated Sugar

Scoop your measuring cup through the granulated sugar until it's formed a heap on top. Level it off with the back of a butter knife.

Brown Sugar

Unless a recipe states otherwise, you can use light brown sugar and dark brown sugar interchangeably. Light brown sugar is the most common kind, while dark brown sugar has a stronger molasses flavor. You'll almost always see recipes call for packed brown sugar, which involves the process of pressing the air pockets out from between those sticky sugar granules as you measure.

How to Manually Measure Brown Sugar

Scoop your measuring cup through the brown sugar and firmly pack it down with your fingers or the back of a spoon. Keep adding and packing the brown sugar until you can level it off with the back of a butter knife. It should hold the shape of the measuring cup when you turn the cup over to empty it.

Powdered Sugar

Powdered sugar is also called confectioner's sugar or icing sugar. Whether or not a recipe calls for sifted powdered sugar, it's best practice to sift it if you see large lumps in it. This will help prevent clumps of powder in an otherwise smooth buttercream.

How to Manually Measure Powdered Sugar

Just like flour, measure powdered sugar by using a spoon to add it to your measuring cup, then level it with the back of a butter knife. If the recipe calls for sifted powdered sugar, follow the same process as detailed in the section on flour.

Cocoa Powder

Natural and Dutch-process are the two most common types of cocoa powder you'll find in baking recipes. If a recipe doesn't specify which type to use, it's safer to default to natural, since Dutch-process has a different chemical makeup and may react differently with the leavening agents in a recipe.

How to Manually Measure Cocoa Powder

Use a spoon to scoop the cocoa powder into your measuring cup, then level it off with the back of a butter knife. If there are large clumps in the cocoa powder, take the time to sift it before measuring, whether or not the recipe calls for it.

Liquid Sweeteners

The liquid sweeteners I'm referring to here include molasses, honey, corn syrup, maple syrup and any kind of thick, sticky liquid.

How to Manually Measure Liquid Sweeteners

Pour the liquid sweetener into a dry measuring cup and use a rubber spatula to scrape what sticks to the cup off into your mixture as you empty the cup. To help with release, you can lightly coat the measuring cup with baking spray before pouring in your sticky ingredients.

Liquids

These ingredients include water, milk, oil, brewed coffee and any kind of true liquid in your ingredients list.

How to Manually Measure Liquids

Pour the liquid into a liquid measuring cup and bend down to eye level to ensure the liquid is resting exactly on the line you're going for.

Semi-liquids

Semi-liquids are ingredients like peanut butter, yogurt, sour cream and anything that's a bit too thick to accurately measure in a liquid measuring cup.

How to Manually Measure Semi-liquids

Use a spoon or rubber spatula to press the ingredient into a dry measuring cup. Press the ingredient down to fill in any air pockets that may be hiding in the bottom of the cup. Release the ingredients with a rubber spatula. To make the release even easier, you can lightly coat the measuring cup with baking spray before adding your semi-liquid ingredient.

Butter

Butter is most often sold in stick form, premeasured to either ½ cup (113 g) or ¼ cup (57 g), with tablespoon increments indicated on the wrapper.

How to Manually Measure Butter

If your butter is in stick form, simply use the guide on the wrapper to measure and slice the amount you need. If your butter is not in stick form, use a dry measuring cup to measure it like you would with any other semi-liquid (see the preceding section for details).

Add-Ins

The add-ins I'm referring to here are ingredients like chocolate chips, berries, sprinkles, crushed cookies, chopped nuts and so on. They're typically added at the end of a recipe.

How to Manually Measure Add-Ins

Scoop add-ins with a dry measuring cup, or pour them into the measuring cup if that's more convenient. Since these ingredients aren't typically used for a cake's structure, there's no need to be ultraprecise.

A   B   C

HOW TO PREPARE CAKE PANS

It's such a joyful moment when you hear the sound of your oven timer and look inside to see beautifully risen cake layers ready to come out—cue the *Hallelujah* chorus! The only thing that can spoil this moment is realizing your cakes are stuck to the pans and won't release without falling apart. No matter how perfectly the baking process goes, it won't end well unless you take the time to properly prepare your cake pans before you pour in the cake batter. Here's my favorite way to prepare cake pans:

STEP 1

Place your empty cake pan on a piece of parchment paper and trace around it with a pencil. Repeat this tracing process per the number of cake layers you plan to bake. Cut out each parchment paper circle using your tracings as a guide (A).

STEP 2

Spray the sides of the pan with baking spray (B; see Tip). This will ensure the sides of the cake won't stick to the pan as it rises and bakes.

TIP:

Baking spray contains a mixture of flour and oil, while cooking spray contains only oil. Both will technically work for greasing cake pans, but baking spray is extra effective for releasing cake layers. If you don't have baking spray or cooking spray on hand, use vegetable oil or butter to coat the sides of the cake pan, then lightly dust the pan with flour.

STEP 3

Place the precut parchment paper on the bottom of the pan (C).

With your cake pans prepared, you're ready to pour in your batter and bake! Just be sure to fill your pans to the specified amount in a recipe. Some recipes will tell you to divide the batter evenly, while others will direct you to fill the pans no more than half or two-thirds full. By paying attention to the pan-filling instructions, you'll avoid overfilling your cake pans and will stand a much better chance of having perfectly risen cake layers.

A　　　　　　　　　B　　　　　　　　　C

RELEASING & COOLING CAKE LAYERS

Once you remove your baked cake layers from the oven, it's essential that you allow them to cool completely before frosting or storing them. Since cake pans retain so much heat, you need to remove the cakes from their pans for best results. Here's how I release and cool my cake layers:

STEP 1

After your cakes are baked, let them cool in the pans for about 5 minutes. Any longer and the sides of the cakes will continue baking from the heat of the pans.

STEP 2

Place a cardboard cake circle or plate over the top of the cake (A). Place your hand on top of the cake circle to create a support for the cake, then flip the pan upside down (B) and slide the pan upward to release the cake (C).

If you find that the cake isn't releasing well, try running a knife between the pan and the cake to release the sides, then turn the pan upside down and release it from the cake. As long as you properly lined the bottom of the pan, the cake layer should release easily. If it doesn't, gently shake the cake pan until the layer releases.

> TIP:
>
> Be sure to protect your hands throughout this entire process—cakes and pans are very hot at this point.

STEP 3

Continue supporting the cake layer as you flip it right side up. Then place it on a wire cooling rack and allow it to cool for at least 2 hours, until it has cooled to room temperature.

CAKE BAKING FAQS & TROUBLESHOOTING GUIDE

At one time or another, you may find that your cake baking session has gone awry. My own cake catastrophes have taught me invaluable lessons in troubleshooting problems, understanding what went wrong and preventing similar situations in the future. In hopes of setting you up for success, I'm sharing my collection of troubleshooting tips for common cake baking issues plus answers to the most frequently asked questions on my blog.

Can I use a handheld mixer instead of a stand mixer?

Absolutely. When mixing cake batter or buttercream with a handheld mixer, be sure to use a large bowl and follow the mixing speeds and times listed in the recipe.

Why did my cake sink in the middle during the baking process?

The cause of this problem can be tricky to pinpoint, because there are a number of reasons. The most common reasons are listed in the following table.

TROUBLESHOOTING A SUNKEN CAKE

Source of the Problem	How to Troubleshoot
The baking powder or baking soda is expired.	Be sure to restock baking powder and baking soda every 6 months.
You overcreamed the butter and sugar.	Set a timer when you begin creaming the butter and sugar, and follow the timing and speed specified in the recipe. If there isn't a time specified, a good rule of thumb is 2 to 4 minutes at medium-high speed. When properly creamed, the butter-sugar mixture will look lighter in color, be fluffy and will have increased in volume.
The butter was too soft.	Butter should be at room temperature, which is ideally between 65 and 68°F (18 to 20°C).
The batter was overmixed.	Use the paddle attachment on your stand mixer and pay attention to mixing speeds and times specified in the recipe. Try using a kitchen timer to ensure you don't mix the batter too long.
The oven was too hot.	See "Working with Your Unique Oven" (page 219) and try using an internal oven thermometer to monitor the temperature.
You made substitutions that aren't working.	See "Common Ingredient Substitutes" (page 215).
The oven door was opened prematurely.	Use the oven light to check on your cakes and do not open the oven door until the minimum time specified in the recipe has elapsed.
Your ingredients weren't at room temperature.	Allow 1 to 2 hours for ingredients to naturally come to room temperature before starting the recipe.

How do I know when a cake is done?

To test a cake for doneness, insert a toothpick or wooden skewer into the center of the cake until it reaches the bottom of the pan, then pull it out. If it comes out clean, the cake is done. If it comes out with wet batter or sticky crumbs on it, the cake needs more time. Here are two other cues for doneness:

1. The edges begin to separate from the sides of the pan.

2. The cake springs back to the touch.

Where should I place the cake pans in the oven?

The middle oven rack is the happy place when it comes to cake baking. It's where the heat sources are most evenly distributed. If you're baking multiple cake layers at once, place the pans a few inches apart and try to avoid placing them too close to the walls of the oven. For example, arrange three pans, spaced 2 to 3 inches (5 to 8 cm) apart, in a triangle formation to avoid the oven's walls.

I have only one cake pan. Can I leave the batter out at room temperature while I bake the individual layers?

Absolutely! While I do recommend investing in multiple cake pans of the same size, you can bake cake layers one at a time. Just be sure to fill the pan no more than two-thirds full before baking and cover the unused batter with a clean kitchen towel while each layer is baking.

Is it okay that my cake layers have domed tops?

Yes, and here's why: As batter bakes and rises, it sets up and becomes cake-like after it has lost a certain amount of moisture. This happens on the edges first because they're next to the side of the pan and in closer contact with direct heat. The middle is the last part of the cake to rise and ends up rising above the sides in the process. To help the cake rise more evenly, you can insulate the sides of the pan with cake strips. If you'd rather not use cake strips, you can easily level the cake layers to remove the domed top (see page 31).

Why did my cake rise unevenly?

Cakes typically rise toward the closest heat source. If the cake rose higher on one side, it's most likely that you placed the cake pan too close to an oven wall, where the heat is more intense. If the cake has a domed top, this is perfectly natural but can be prevented by insulating the sides of your pan with cake strips. If the cake sunk in the middle, see the troubleshooting tips in the table titled "Troubleshooting a Sunken Cake" on page 23.

Can I salvage a sunken cake layer?

If your cake layers have sunken in the middle after baking, consult the table titled "Troubleshooting a Sunken Cake" on page 23 to determine what the problem might have been, then try leveling the cake layer (see page 31) to cut off the uneven top. As long as the cake layer is baked through, you should be able to salvage it.

How should I store baked cake layers?

First, make sure the cakes are completely cool to the touch. Then either wrap them in plastic wrap and store them at room temperature for up to 2 days, or wrap them in an additional layer of aluminum foil and freeze them in an airtight container for up to 2 months.

Is there a quicker way to cool cake layers than letting them rest at room temperature?

I don't recommend placing warm cakes in the refrigerator or freezer to speed up the cooling process—the extreme temperature change can shock the cake and create extra condensation. If you're in a real pinch, you can certainly try it, but be aware that exposed cake layers in the refrigerator or freezer can dry out. Instead, I recommend being patient with the cooling process or planning to make your cakes ahead of time, whether it's a day ahead or a month ahead.

How do I scale a recipe up or down?

Scaling a recipe will involve some math. Here are some quick tips:

- To scale a recipe down (e.g., to cut it in half, thirds or quarters), divide all of the ingredients by the scaling amount. For example, to halve a recipe, divide all of the ingredients by two.

- To scale a recipe up (e.g., to double it, triple it and so on), multiply all of the ingredients by the scaling amount. For example, to double a recipe, multiply all of the ingredients by two.

- If you end up with an odd number of eggs, crack an egg into a bowl and whisk it before dividing it into the amount you need. For example, if you need one-third of an egg and the beaten egg totals 3 tablespoons (45 ml), use 1 tablespoon (15 ml). If you need 2½ eggs, use 2 whole eggs plus half of a beaten egg.

Chapter 2
HOW TO BUILD A LAYER CAKE

After baking your cakes and preparing all your frostings and fillings (and sampling a few bites, of course), it's easy to get excited and want to jump right into decorating. But if you don't take the time to build a strong foundation for your layer cake, that decorating you're dreaming of can quickly go from fun to fiasco. Misshapen cakes, bulging layers and sinking decorations are actually all prevented here in the cake building process.

There are many things to take into consideration when building your layer cake, but don't let that fact overwhelm you. Just like the rest of the basics, once you learn these techniques, they'll quickly become second nature. In this chapter, we'll look at everything you need to know about the cake building process: from the time the cake layers have cooled to the time you apply that final layer of frosting and prepare to decorate. You'll learn to consider the weight of your cake layers, the consistency of your fillings and frostings, the temperature of your kitchen and, of course, the ever-present reality of gravity. In this chapter, you'll learn how to create the perfect blank canvas so that your cake designs can shine.

ANATOMY OF A
LAYER CAKE

CAKE LAYER

Creating Level Layers (page 31)

FILLING

Filling & Stacking (page 32)

CRUMB COAT

Crumb Coating (page 37)

EXTERIOR DECORATION

Chocolate Ganache Drip (page 97)
Swirl Border (page 116)
Sprinkles (page 105)

A   B   C

CREATING LEVEL LAYERS

If you cut into any layer cake that looks beautiful on the outside, chances are you'll find perfectly even, uniform cake layers on the inside. But in the baking process, cakes don't always come out of the oven perfectly level. Some bake up flat while others form domed tops as they rise in the oven. One layer might bake up a little taller than the others in your batch. The secret to making those layers equally tall, perfectly flat, aesthetically pleasing and easy to stack? A magical little process called leveling.

Leveling is the process of creating uniformity among your cake layers by cutting off any uneven tops. It's not only important for creating picturesque cake slices, it's actually essential for building a strong layer cake foundation. I recommend having a cake leveler on hand for this process, but alternatively you can use a serrated knife to get the job done.

HOW TO LEVEL CAKE LAYERS

STEP 1

Set a cardboard cake round on a flat surface and place the cake layer on top. Hold your cake leveler next to the layer and adjust the wire blade to your desired height (A). Everything above the blade will be trimmed off.

If you're using a serrated knife, hold the knife horizontally next to the cake layer where you'd like to trim. Rotate the cake layer, with the blade pressed lightly against the cake, to score it with a faint line. Make sure to keep the knife at the same height all around.

> **TIP:**
>
> Use the shortest cake layer to measure with the cake leveler. This will ensure that all the cake layers end up the same height after leveling.

STEP 2

Support the cake layer with one hand while you use a gentle sawing motion with the other to slice through the cake (B). Make sure to keep the feet of the cake leveler on a flat surface the entire time.

STEP 3

Remove the top of the cake layer (C). If you used a serrated knife and the cake doesn't look as level as you want, continue trimming with the knife until it looks even.

Repeat this process for any additional cake layers before moving on to filling and stacking or storing them for later use.

FILLING & STACKING

If cake layers were the bricks in a building, the filling would be the mortar. Unlike mortar, though, which is designed to uphold the weight of a brick against gravity, not all fillings are the right consistency to uphold the weight of a cake layer. A filling that is too thin will bulge or even ooze out from between cake layers as gravity takes hold. Cake layers can easily shift around if the filling between them isn't sturdy enough, making the final outcome lopsided. To avoid fiascos like these, it's critical to know how to work with different filling consistencies as you stack your way to a strong layer cake foundation.

There are two main consistencies of cake fillings: stable fillings like buttercream and soft fillings like ganache, jam, salted caramel and lemon curd. Taking gravity and structural engineering into consideration, the following pages show my favorite methods for filling and stacking a triple-layer cake with either type of filling.

USING BUTTERCREAM AS FILLING

Filling a cake with buttercream is straightforward as long as you're working with the right consistency of buttercream (page 44). All of the buttercream recipes you'll find in this book should conveniently be the perfect consistency for filling, crumb coating and frosting a layer cake.

STEP 1

Place a cardboard cake circle that's the same diameter as your cake layers on a turntable. Then swipe a small dab of buttercream onto the cake circle before adding the first cake layer on top (A). This little swipe of buttercream acts as glue to keep the bottom layer in place.

STEP 2

Add about ¾ cup (161 g) of buttercream to the cake layer (B) and smooth it down with an angled spatula as you rotate the turntable (C). Keep smoothing the buttercream filling, adding more if needed, until it is about ½ inch (1.3 cm) thick, it is level and it reaches slightly beyond the edge of the cake layer.

STEP 3

Place the second cake layer on top of the buttercream filling, lining up the edges of the second layer with those of the first layer (D). Gently press down on top of the cake layer to adhere it to the buttercream. Repeat step 2 (E).

STEP 4

Add the final cake layer on top, upside down so that the bottom of the final cake layer becomes the top of the cake (F). You can now move on to crumb coating!

TIP:

No matter how many layers your cake has, the very top cake layer should always be placed upside down.

USING SOFT FILLINGS

Using softer fillings like chocolate ganache, lemon curd, salted caramel and anything that could easily spread under the weight of a cake layer requires creating additional structure. My favorite way to do this is with a buttercream dam—a piped circle of buttercream on the edge of the cake layer that keeps your filling contained in the stacking process. Here's how to use a buttercream dam with a soft filling:

STEP 1

Place a cardboard cake circle that's the same diameter as your cake layers on a turntable. Then swipe a small dab of buttercream onto the cake circle before placing the first cake layer on top of the buttercream (A). This little swipe of buttercream acts as glue to keep the bottom layer in place.

STEP 2

Fill a piping bag with medium- or stiff-consistency buttercream (page 44). Use scissors to snip off a ½-inch (1.3-cm) opening in the piping bag. The buttercream you'll be using to crumb coat and frost the cake will work as it is or as a starting point for thickening, if necessary.

> TIP:
>
> The firmer the buttercream, the more structurally sound the buttercream dam will be, but be sure to keep flavor in mind. Stiff buttercream requires more powdered sugar, so it's important to taste as you go and balance the sweetness with a little salt.

STEP 3

Place the piping bag about ¼ inch (6 mm) inward from the edge of the cake layer. Then rotate the turntable with one hand as you pipe the buttercream along the outer edge to create a circle (B), keeping about ¼ inch (6 mm) of distance between the edge of the cake layer and the buttercream as you go along.

STEP 4

Place about ½ cup (120 g) of filling inside the buttercream dam (C). Spread and smooth down the filling with an angled spatula, adding more filling if needed, until it's level with the height of the buttercream dam and fills the entire center of the cake (D).

STEP 5

Place the second cake layer on top of the filling, lining up the edges of the second layer with those of the bottom cake layer (E). Gently press down on top of the second cake layer to adhere it to the filling. Repeat steps 3 and 4.

STEP 6

Place the final cake layer on top (F) upside down so that the bottom of the final cake layer becomes the top of the cake. You're now ready to head to the next page for crumb coating!

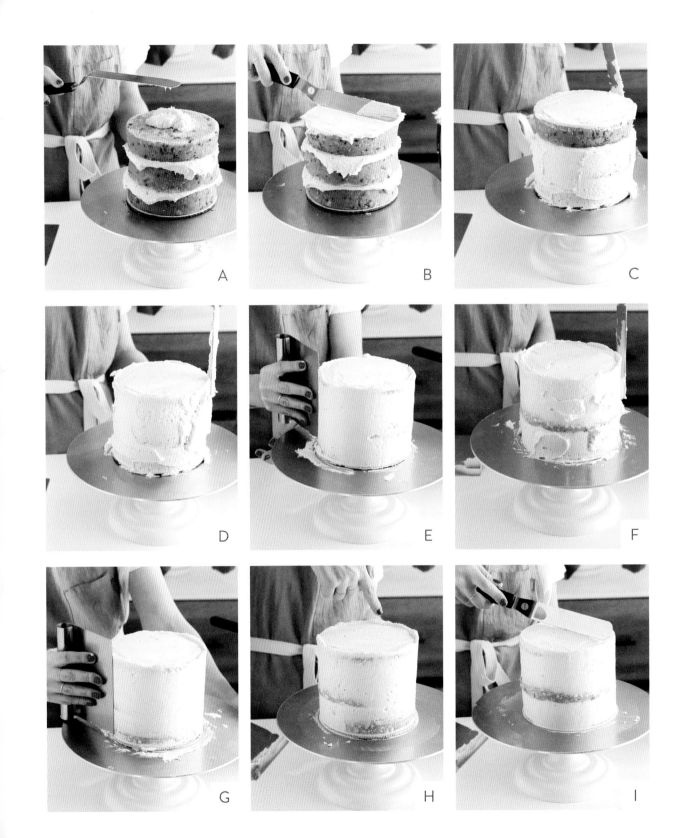

CRUMB COATING

In the cake building process, it's tempting to start frosting the cake as soon as you finish filling and stacking the layers. If you jump ahead to frosting the cake right now, you'll wind up with messy crumbs in your cake frosting and risk your cake layers shifting around while you decorate. Talk about stressful.

Luckily, there's a solution. Crumb coating helps you create a strong foundation for your frosting and decorating: A crumb coating catches any loose cake crumbs that want to sneak their way into your beautiful buttercream finish, and it creates a smooth, even surface to ensure your cake is level for your final layer of buttercream.

All beautiful cake finishes begin with a solid crumb coat foundation. Trust me—don't skip this step. The following section shows how to apply your crumb coat.

HOW TO CRUMB COAT A CAKE

STEP 1

Begin by putting about 1 cup (215 g) of frosting in a small bowl. This is what you'll use to crumb coat your cake instead of dipping your spatula into the larger bowl of frosting. Now place your freshly filled and stacked cake on a turntable.

STEP 2

Add a few dollops of buttercream to the top of your cake (A) and smooth the frosting down with an angled spatula to create an even layer that is about ⅛ inch (3 mm) thick (B).

STEP 3

Using an angled spatula, add the remaining buttercream to the sides of the cake, working from the bottom up (C, D). When the sides are covered, hold an icing smoother at a 45-degree angle toward you while simultaneously rotating the turntable and smoothing the frosting down (E).

After each rotation, use the edge of your frosting bowl to scrape the excess buttercream off of your icing smoother. This keeps the icing smoother and clean for each go-round.

When pausing to scrape your icing smoother, you may notice that you have patchy areas in the buttercream where there isn't much frosting. Fill in these areas with more buttercream (F). Keep repeating the process of smoothing and patching until you've got a level crumb coat on the sides of the cake (G).

STEP 4

Since you've been concentrating on the sides, you'll notice that a frosting "crown" has formed around the top edges of your cake (H). That's okay! This is what should be happening. Using a clean angled spatula, swipe the crowned edges toward the center of the cake's top layer to create sharp edges (I).

STEP 5

When your cake is level and covered in a nice, thin crumb coat, pop the whole thing—turntable and all—into the refrigerator to chill for at least 30 minutes. If you're short on time, you can chill the crumb-coated cake in the freezer for 15 minutes. The chilling process allows the frosting to firm up and create a solid foundation for the final layer of frosting.

A FINAL NOTE

After chilling your crumb-coated cake, you're now ready to move on to your final layer of frosting and decorating—hooray! You'll find decorating tutorials and ideas in Chapter 3 (page 41). If you need to pause here for the day, it's perfectly fine to refrigerate a crumb-coated cake overnight. Even though the crumb coat is thin, it still helps preserve the cake layers beneath, keeping them moist and fresh.

LAYER CAKE FAQS & TROUBLESHOOTING GUIDE

Building layer cakes will become second nature the more you practice. Still, there may be times where you need to troubleshoot in order to create the perfect layer cake foundation. For those times you need a little extra help, here's my collection of troubleshooting tips for common issues plus answers to the most frequently asked questions on my blog regarding this topic.

How tall are your cakes?

My go-to height is three layers of cake with filling between the layers. This means my layer cakes are between 5 and 6 inches (13 and 15 cm) tall.

What if I want to build an extra tall cake?

The higher you fill and stack your cakes, the less sturdy they will become due to the weight of the layers and the nature of gravity. If you want to make an extra tall cake (which I define as five or more layers), I recommend filling and stacking two shorter cakes and inserting wooden dowels or plastic boba straws into the bottom cake before placing the second one on top. The dowels should be cut to the exact height of the bottom cake and placed to uphold the cardboard cake circle that the top cake is built on, preventing the whole structure from collapsing under the weight of gravity (A).

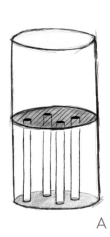 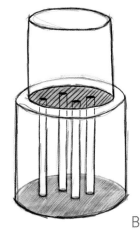

A   B

How do I build a tiered cake?

You'll use the same dowel support system as described in the previous question, except that you'll place the dowels in such a way that they support the slightly smaller cake tier above (B).

What should I do if my fillings start to bulge?

A bit of bulge should be fine if it can be covered up with a crumb coat and a final layer of frosting, so let the cake settle as much as it's going to before popping it into the refrigerator to let everything firm up. From here, you can take a knife to the bulges and trim them slightly if necessary. Then move on to crumb coating or decorating if the crumb coat has already been applied.

How do I prevent the filling bulge next time?

Use a firmer buttercream as a dam around any softer fillings (see page 35). It should be firm enough to support the weight of the cake layer above and placed slightly inward from the edge of the cake layer it's piped on. This placement will allow for some room for the buttercream dam to spread slightly when the next layer is placed on top.

What should I do if the icing begins tearing the cake while I'm crumb coating?

This happens because your icing is too thick. You'll need to thin out the buttercream's consistency (page 44) so that the icing glides over the cake and locks in the crumbs instead of tearing the cake and creating more crumbs.

What should I do if my cake becomes lopsided while I'm crumb coating?

This usually happens due to the filling not being stable enough or your kitchen environment being too warm, but it can be fixed. Working quickly, gently shift the layers with your hands until the cake looks level, and then use a gentle touch while finishing the crumb coating process so you don't easily shift the layers. Once the cake is crumb coated and looking level, pop it into the refrigerator so it sets to retain its shape.

Chapter 3
CAKE DECORATING IDEAS & TECHNIQUES

The processes of baking and building layer cakes are art forms in their own ways, but decorating is where creativity really comes alive. An eye-catching color palette, thoughtful design and decorative finishing touches can transform an ordinary layer cake into something truly memorable.

While decorating is the part of the cake-making process that takes the most patience, I am a firm believer that with the right tools, the correct techniques and a willingness to practice, anyone can make beautiful cakes regardless of their current skill level. Perhaps you feel a little intimidated at the thought of decorating and don't (yet) consider yourself an artist. That's okay! After applying what you learn here, it's only a matter of time before you end up surprising yourself.

The methods you'll read about in this chapter are the ones I swear by for all of my layer cakes: frosting a smooth cake, making picture-perfect ganache drips, applying artistic textures, using jaw-dropping color palettes and so much more. There is nothing cake-related that brings me more joy than helping you make your cakes look as irresistible as they taste. My hope is that, as you master these techniques, you'll find yourself confident and liberated as you decorate. Maybe even so liberated that you crank up some music and dance around the kitchen a little—or a lot.

1

2

3

4

5

6

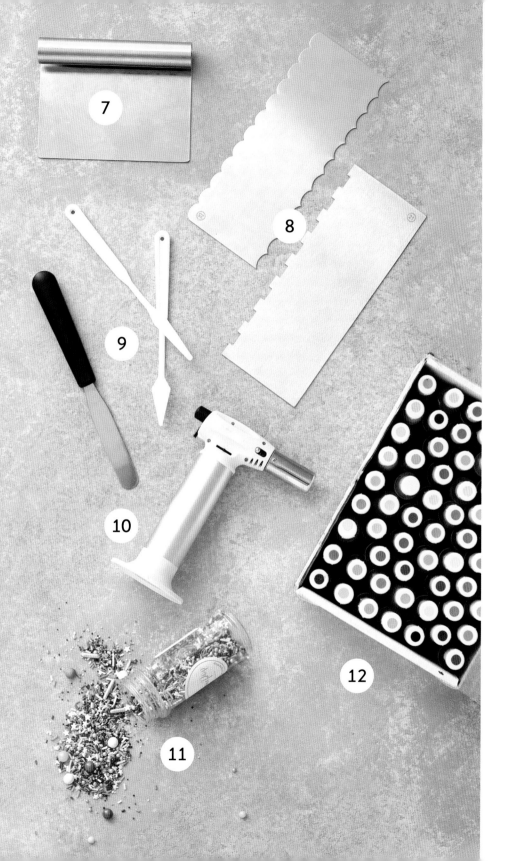

1. Turntable

2. Cake Rounds

3. Cake Leveler

4. Piping Bags

5. Piping Tips

6. Angled Spatula

7. Icing Smoother

8. Icing Combs

9. Small Icing Spatula or Palette Knife

10. Kitchen Torch

11. Sprinkles

12. Gel Food Coloring

You'll find a list of my favorite brands for all of these decorating tools at sugarandsparrow.com/tools.

BUTTERCREAM FROSTING CONSISTENCY

When it comes to working with buttercream frosting, knowing how to alter the consistency for different tasks is a game changer. For example, if you're piping with buttercream that is too soft, your decorations won't hold their shape quite as well as if you were using a stiffer buttercream. If you're frosting a cake with buttercream that is too stiff, it won't smooth out easily, leaving the texture rough and blotchy. Either extreme can be incredibly frustrating.

Luckily, once you know what to do, changing the consistency is easy, even after your buttercream has been made. Here are some examples of different buttercream consistencies, when to use them and how to make them.

MEDIUM CONSISTENCY

The buttercream recipes in this book are all medium consistency by default. Medium is the most versatile of the three consistencies. It's ideal for using as buttercream filling, creating a dam for soft fillings, adding a crumb coating, frosting the finish and piping simple decorations like swirls, stars and borders.

THIN CONSISTENCY

If your buttercream feels so thick that it's ripping the cake when you're trying to crumb coat it or you're having a hard time achieving a smooth frosting finish with medium consistency, I recommend thinning out the buttercream. You can do this by placing the amount of buttercream you'd like to thin in the bowl of your stand mixer and adding room-temperature milk, 2 teaspoons (10 ml) for every 1 cup (215 g) of buttercream, while mixing at low speed. You'll know you've got thin consistency when the buttercream forms soft peaks when you dip your spatula into it and it's very easy to spread.

STIFF CONSISTENCY

Stiff buttercream is the best consistency to use for piping intricate things like buttercream flowers and other decorations that have upright elements. To stiffen your buttercream, gradually add more powdered sugar, 2 to 3 tablespoons (16 to 24 g) of powdered sugar at a time, until you have a thick yet pipeable consistency. You can mix the powdered sugar in by hand with a rubber spatula or combine it with your buttercream in a stand mixer running at low speed. It should maintain a stiff peak when you dip your spatula into it.

FINAL NOTES ABOUT BUTTERCREAM CONSISTENCY

Following are a few important notes on altering your buttercream consistency:

Keep in mind that if you add powdered sugar to your buttercream to stiffen the consistency, the sugar will make the frosting sweeter. Taste the buttercream as you go, and balance the sweetness with a little salt if you need to.

The temperature of your kitchen directly affects the overall consistency of your buttercream. The frosting begins to soften and thin out when your environment is above 75°F (24°C). Instead of adding more powdered sugar in a situation like this, I recommend placing the entire batch of buttercream in the refrigerator for 10 to 15 minutes, then remixing it with your stand mixer. This will allow the butter in the recipe to firm up and stabilize the consistency to make it easier to work with.

If you live in a particularly warm climate, consider altering your buttercream recipe to make it more heat-stable. Page 121 explains my recommendation.

BUTTERCREAM FROSTING
CONSISTENCY GUIDE

THIN CONSISTENCY

MEDIUM CONSISTENCY

STIFF CONSISTENCY

YOUR GUIDE TO

COLORING BUTTERCREAM

A huge part of carrying out your creative vision with cake design is getting your buttercream color palette to look like what you have pictured in your mind. As with anything, getting buttercream hues just right involves practice and finding products that work best for you. This guide will show you how I mix buttercream colors, whiten buttercream and make dark colors like black.

FIVE TIPS FOR SUCCESS

Here are five tips that will help ensure that you end up with beautiful buttercream.

1. Consider the Buttercream Type

Buttercream type makes a huge difference in color outcome. I use American buttercream for my cakes, which is very easy to color and achieves rich hues without requiring a lot of colorant. Other types of buttercream, such as Swiss meringue or other meringue-based buttercreams, don't take color as easily because their high fat content is not as compatible with water-based gels. If you're working with those types of buttercream, you may need to experiment with oil-based gels, powdered food coloring or alternative coloring methods.

2. Use High-Quality Products

Not all food coloring is made equal. To make sure you don't alter the flavor or consistency of your buttercream, you'll need to use products that are powerful enough to color buttercream and other foods without sacrificing the quality or taste. My favorite products for creating colorful cakes are these:

AmeriColor® Soft Gel Paste™. These food coloring gels come in every color imaginable and are highly concentrated, so you don't have to use a lot—plus, they're formulated in such a way that they won't affect the flavor or consistency of your buttercream.

Wilton Color Right Performance Color System. This is a pack of eight different food coloring gels that you can mix and match to create any color you want. They come with a color chart to guide you in your color mixing, and once you get the hang of color theory (page 55), you'll be a pro at making the buttercream hues you envision.

3.   **Start with the Right Base Color**

When coloring buttercream, it's important to know that whatever color the buttercream is to start with (a.k.a. the base color) will mix with any color you add, which has an impact on the final color. To get the purest colors, you'll want to start with a white frosting like Vanilla Buttercream (page 133). If you're going for a dark-colored buttercream, start with a darker frosting recipe like Chocolate Buttercream (page 132). It's much easier to go from brown to black and so on than it is to go from white to black.

4.   **Start Small**

The smaller amount of buttercream you start with, the smaller the amount of color gel you'll need to use to get a rich color. That being said, if you're going for a pastel color and starting with a small amount, it's also easy to add too much color gel and go overboard. Once you have the amount of buttercream measured out, the best way to approach coloring buttercream is to start with a small amount of gel, fully mix it in, see what color you end up with and add more as needed.

5.   **Allow Time for Colors to Deepen**

Not only does the color get richer as you add more gel, but the color will actually darken a little more over time. Some colors may look much more intense when left alone overnight.

BEFORE

AFTER

HOW TO MAKE BRIGHT WHITE BUTTERCREAM

You may be thinking, *Isn't vanilla buttercream already white?* Not exactly. Since buttercream is made with butter, which is yellow, the frosting tends to be more of a cream color. This might look white at first, but it will subtly add a slight yellow tint to the frosting color you choose. To make buttercream pure white, you can use a flavorless icing whitener. Add about ½ teaspoon at a time until you achieve bright white buttercream. I love AmeriColor Soft Gel Paste in Bright White for this, because it's so concentrated that it doesn't take more than about 1 teaspoon per batch of buttercream to get a brilliant white color.

TIP:

Keep an eye on the consistency of the buttercream as you add icing whitener. Since it's a thick liquid, you'll essentially be adding more liquid to the batch of frosting. This may start to thin out the buttercream consistency if you add too much.

HOW TO MAKE BLACK BUTTERCREAM

If you've ever tried to turn a big batch of vanilla buttercream black using only food coloring, you know that it takes a lot of coloring—so much that it not only can ruin the flavor and consistency of your buttercream but can also make eating the cake less fun because everyone is left with stained teeth and tongues afterward. Instead, start with Chocolate Buttercream (page 132), which is naturally darker.

STEP 1

Make the Chocolate Buttercream recipe on page 132, but use ¼ cup (23 g) of black cocoa powder and ¼ cup (23 g) of natural unsweetened cocoa powder in place of the ½ cup (45 g) of natural unsweetened cocoa powder called for in the ingredients list (A).

> **TIP:**
>
> If you can't find black cocoa powder, you can use the Chocolate Buttercream recipe as is. You'll just need to double the amount of food coloring gel in step 2.

STEP 2

Add ¾ teaspoon of AmeriColor Soft Gel Paste in Super Black or another very concentrated black food coloring gel (B), and then mix the buttercream at low speed for 1 to 2 minutes, until the color is uniform. The color will look like wet concrete at this stage (C).

STEP 3

Place the buttercream in an airtight container and store it for at least 24 hours. This is the amount of time it takes for the color to transform from a deep gray to black. If you're storing it for only 24 hours, you can set the container out at room temperature. Any longer and you'll need to store the black buttercream in the refrigerator, where it will last for up to 2 weeks.

STEP 4

After 24 hours or more, bring the buttercream to room temperature if necessary and place it in the bowl of your stand mixer. Mix the buttercream at low speed for 1 to 2 minutes, until the consistency is smooth and uniform (D).

A

B

C

HOW TO MAKE ANY BUTTERCREAM COLOR

Okay, that title is slightly misleading—I won't be giving you ratios for every possible color. Instead, allow me to guide you through some rules about color theory to visually show you how colors mix and change when you combine them. With this knowledge, you'll be able to aim for the colors you truly want and will be more confident when faced with a fresh bowl of buttercream.

I recommend practicing with Vanilla Buttercream (page 133) if you want to produce lighter and saturated colors. If you want to create darker colors, make my Chocolate Buttercream (page 132).

STEP 1

Place the amount of buttercream you'd like to color in a bowl (A). If you're coloring an entire batch of buttercream, it's easiest to keep it in the bowl of your stand mixer.

STEP 2

Place a very small amount of color gel on a toothpick, then dip the toothpick into the bowl of buttercream (B). Mix it all together thoroughly and take note of what color you've made (C).

STEP 3

Repeat step 2 until you've created the color you're going for, using the following pages as your guide.

BUTTERCREAM COLOR WHEEL

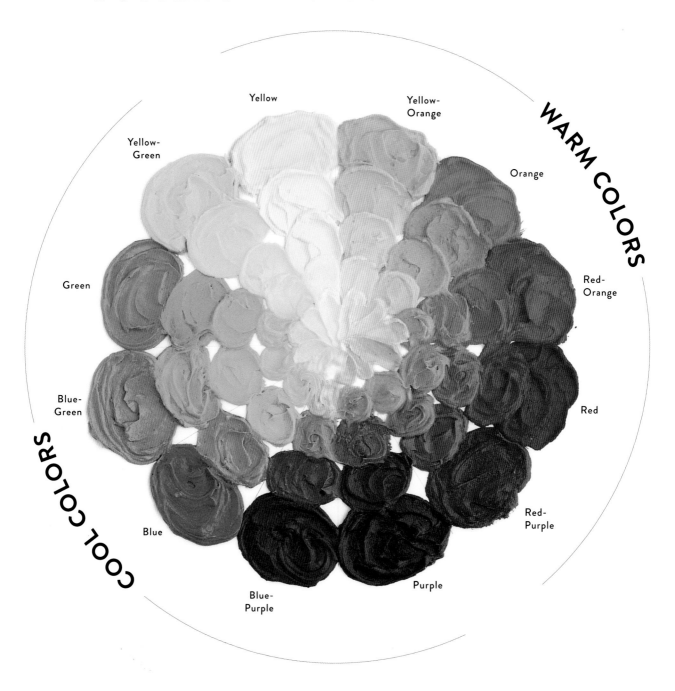

Yellow

Yellow-Orange

Yellow-Green

Orange

WARM COLORS

Red-Orange

Green

Red

Blue-Green

Red-Purple

COOL COLORS

Blue

Blue-Purple

Purple

BUTTERCREAM COLOR THEORY

Making beautiful buttercream colors is less about having an exact recipe and more about knowing how colors change when mixed with other colors. Following are some helpful charts and concepts to inspire you.

COLOR INTENSITY

The more color gel you add to your buttercream, the more saturated or intense the color will end up. Here is a visual example of how color changes as more color gel is added.

COLOR TEMPERATURE

If I asked five different people to make purple buttercream, we would end up with five different purples. What's interesting is that these purples would naturally fall into warmer or cooler tones. This range of colors is called color temperature, and because there is no one universal temperature for any given color, the temperature can really affect the overall hue. Changing the temperature of any color can be accomplished by mixing in a tiny bit of a cool-toned primary color (blue) or a warm-toned primary color (red or yellow). Take a look at the swatches in the following image to see how the color purple changes from cool to warm as I mix in varying amounts of blue and red:

TIP:

Buttercream colors usually intensify over time as well, especially when you're mixing very dark colors like black (page 51).

TIP:

When adjusting color temperature, always start with the smallest amount of warm- or cool-toned primary color so you don't overdo it. Sometimes it's good to try it with a small sample of buttercream so you don't mess up an entire batch.

HOW TO LIGHTEN COLORS

Here are two ways to lighten colors when you add too much color gel:

1. Add more white buttercream.

2. Mix in a drop or two of AmeriColor Soft Gel Paste in Bright White until the desired color is reached.

HOW TO DARKEN COLORS

Colors can be darkened by adding black color gel in very small amounts until the desired color is reached.

COLOR-MIXING CHART

The next page shows some of my favorite buttercream colors to mix up. You'll notice that there is no exact recipe for each color—this is because the amount of color gel added will vary depending on the volume of buttercream you're tinting. Instead, I've included the measurements in parts. When you see an equation such as 3 parts pink plus 1 part brown, you can equate this to 3 drops of pink plus 1 drop of brown and scale those amounts up for larger amounts of buttercream or down for smaller amounts of buttercream. Remember, starting with a small amount of color gel is one of the keys to success when you're creating buttercream colors. After you mix in the color gel and observe the color you create, you can continue adding and altering the color gel additions from there.

As you practice and become more confident with buttercream and your coloring techniques, you'll be able to mix up any color you can think of!

FUCHSIA
4 parts pink + 1 part purple

BLOOD ORANGE
2 parts red + 1 part orange

DUSTY ROSE
2 parts pink + 1 part brown

CORAL
2 parts pink + 1 part orange

PEACH
3 parts red + 4 parts yellow

BURNT ORANGE
2 parts orange + 1 part brown

MUSTARD YELLOW
2 parts yellow + 1 part brown

SEAFOAM GREEN
1 part yellow + 1 part blue +
1 part brown

AVOCADO
2 parts green + 1 part brown

FOREST GREEN
2 parts green + 1 part black

TURQUOISE
1 part blue + 1 part green

SKY BLUE
8 parts blue + 1 part yellow

PERIWINKLE
2 parts blue + 1 part purple

NAVY BLUE
1 part blue + 1 part black

LAVENDER
2 parts purple + 1 part pink

DEEP PURPLE
4 parts red + 2 parts pink +
2 parts blue

EGGPLANT
4 parts red + 3 parts blue +
1 part black

GRAY
Add 1 drop black until desired
shade is reached

FROSTING
FINISH TUTORIALS

You've learned how to bake the perfect cake layers, fill and stack them into a stable foundation, lock in the layers with a good crumb coat and prepare your buttercream for decorating. Now it's time to get creative with that final layer of frosting! Your frosting finish can either be the blank canvas for additional decorations or the focal point of the whole cake. Regardless, this layer of frosting marks the starting point for the rest of your design.

The next several pages will show you how to achieve a variety of styles, from an ultra-smooth buttercream finish to rustic texture, painterly techniques, buttercream stripes and even some classic vintage-inspired looks. Combine these tutorials with any of my recipes in Chapter 4 (page 123) or Chapter 5 (page 143), and feel free to get creative with the color schemes and additional finishing touches—the possibilities are endless!

SMOOTH
BUTTERCREAM

A smooth buttercream finish is my go-to for all sorts of cake designs. It looks beautiful in any color and can be paired with many artistic styles to create captivating cakes. This gives you the best baseline finish to add further decoration on top without having to worry about unique textures getting in the way. I know how daunting smoothing a cake can be if you've never tried or if you've struggled with this technique in the past. I've struggled too! After so many years of practice, though, I've learned a few things that help make the process quicker, easier and more seamless—literally!

TOOLS & MATERIALS

A cake that's been crumb coated (page 37) and chilled for at least 30 minutes

Turntable

Angled spatula

3 cups (645 g) medium-consistency buttercream

Icing smoother

TIPS FOR SUCCESS

Use a medium-consistency buttercream (page 44) to start with, and consider thinning out the consistency for step 6 if you need to.

Clean your icing smoother and angled spatula between turns, either by scraping off excess buttercream on the rim of the frosting bowl or wiping it off with a paper towel.

If you find yourself struggling with step 3 or step 4, try gently warming your icing smoother by running it under hot water. Dry it completely with a kitchen towel before smoothing the buttercream. Just like a hot iron helps remove wrinkles from clothing, a heated icing smoother can help smooth out imperfections. Be careful with heat, though—too much can melt the buttercream.

If you start stressing out, rest assured that step 6 should solve everything!

SMOOTH BUTTERCREAM TUTORIAL

STEP 1

With the chilled, crumb-coated cake on the turntable, use an angled spatula to add about ⅓ cup (72 g) of buttercream in dollops to the top of the cake (A). Smooth and flatten the buttercream by holding the angled spatula parallel to the top of the cake as you rotate the turntable. Keep adding and smoothing the buttercream until it's about ¼ inch (6 mm) thick and reaches over the top edge of the cake (B).

STEP 2

Using the angled spatula, apply about ¼ inch (6 mm) of buttercream to the sides of the cake, working from the bottom up until you reach the top (C).

STEP 3

Once the sides of the cake are completely covered, hold the icing smoother next to the cake. You'll want to make sure the icing smoother is as vertically straight as possible and at a very tight angle to the cake. The tighter the angle, the better the excess buttercream fills the gaps as it's pulled around the cake.

Position your free hand on the turntable in front of the cake (D) and rotate the turntable as you hold the icing smoother in place (E). The fuller your rotation of the turntable, the more seamless the sides will look. Scrape the excess buttercream from your icing smoother onto the rim of the frosting bowl after each turn.

STEP 4

Fill any gaps and imperfections with more buttercream (F) and repeat the smoothing technique in step 3 as many times as you need (G).

STEP 5

Once your sides are smooth, you should notice a crown of buttercream that has formed along the top edge of the cake (H). This is what you want! Turn the angled spatula 90 degrees and swipe the crown of buttercream inward, toward the center of the cake, to create sharp edges all around the top (I).

STEP 6 (OPTIONAL)

If you feel that your buttercream finish isn't as smooth as you want it to be, there's an easy solution! Pop the entire cake, turntable and all, back into the refrigerator for 20 to 30 minutes, until the frosting firms up. Then, repeat steps 1 through 5 with a very thin layer of buttercream. This will fill in all of the imperfections in the cake's finish and make the smoothing process a breeze due to a solid foundation of cold buttercream beneath.

SEMI-
NAKED

This "barely there" finish has a beautiful rustic look. It involves a very thin layer of buttercream (hence the name), making it the quickest and easiest finish to replicate. Pair it with a decorative drip (page 97), some fresh fruit or a few food-safe flowers and you'll have a gorgeous event cake that's easy as can be.

TOOLS & MATERIALS

A cake that's been crumb coated (page 37) and chilled for at least 30 minutes

Turntable

Angled spatula

1–2 cups (215–430 g) thin-consistency buttercream

Icing smoother

TIPS FOR SUCCESS

When you crumb coat the cake prior to this technique, be sure to use as little buttercream as possible, just enough to catch the crumbs and fill in any imperfections.

Since you'll be adding such a thin layer of buttercream as a final layer, use a gentle touch when smoothing it. The goal is to let portions of the cake layers peek through the buttercream without digging into the crumb coat.

SEMI-NAKED TUTORIAL

With the chilled, crumb-coated cake on the turntable, use an angled spatula to add ⅓ cup (72 g) of buttercream in dollops to the top of the cake (A). Smooth and flatten the buttercream by holding the angled spatula parallel to the top of the cake as you rotate the turntable. Keep adding and smoothing the buttercream until it's about ¼ inch (6 mm) thick and reaches over the top edge of the cake (B).

STEP 2

Using the angled spatula, apply a thin layer of buttercream, about ⅛ inch (3 mm) thick, to the sides of the cake, working from the bottom up until you reach the top (C).

STEP 3

Once the sides of the cake are completely covered, hold the icing smoother next to the cake at roughly a 45-degree angle (D). Rotate the turntable as you hold the icing smoother in place (E). Use a gentle touch as you do this—the goal is to remove as much of the buttercream as possible without exposing crumbs or scraping into the cake layers. Clean your icing smoother after each turn by scraping the excess buttercream onto the rim of the frosting bowl.

STEP 4

Fill any gaps by adding more buttercream and continue smoothing until you see portions of the cake layers peeking through the frosting and the overall finish looks smooth and level (F, G).

STEP 5

Turn the angled spatula 90 degrees and swipe the crown of buttercream inward, toward the center of the cake, to create sharp edges (H). Repeat this step until you create sharp edges all around the top of the cake (I).

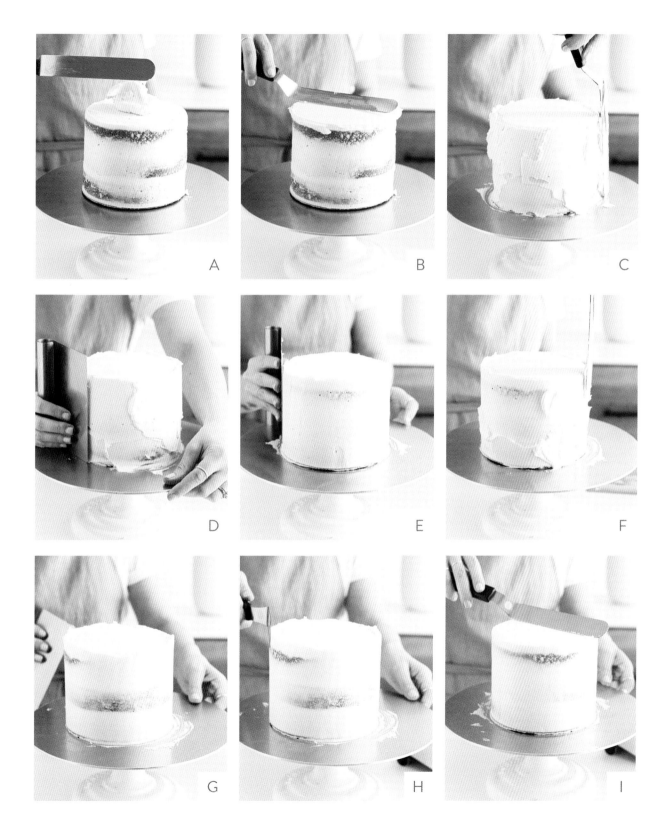

IMPRESSIONIST

Inspired by the painting style made famous by artists such as Claude Monet and Pierre-Auguste Renoir, this frosting finish looks amazing in all sorts of color palettes. A smooth buttercream finish makes the perfect blank canvas for this elegant yet approachable texture.

TOOLS & MATERIALS

1–2 cups (215–430 g) medium-consistency buttercream

Bowls and spoons for color mixing

Food coloring gels of your choice

A cake that's been frosted smooth (page 61) and chilled for at least 30 minutes

Turntable

Small icing spatula or palette knife

Paper towels

TIPS FOR SUCCESS

Use medium-consistency buttercream for both the smooth buttercream finish and the spatula-painted portions.

To give this look the most depth, use at least five different colors for the spatula-painted portions.

This design works great with a palette of different colors but is also striking with a few different shades of the same color (i.e., a monochromatic palette).

IMPRESSIONIST TUTORIAL

STEP 1

Create your buttercream color palette. Divide the buttercream evenly between individual bowls and add food coloring gel to each bowl of frosting. Use a separate spoon to mix each color into the buttercream until you've created your desired color palette.

TIP:

For color-mixing instructions and inspiration, see "Your Guide to Coloring Buttercream" (pages 47–57).

STEP 2

With the chilled cake on the turntable, use a single color of buttercream and a small icing spatula or palette knife to make swipes of buttercream that are no longer than ½ inch (1.3 cm) on the top and top third of the cake in a random placement (A). Place just a few swipes on the bottom two-thirds of the cake (B). The goal is to make the color swipes more concentrated on the top third of the cake and gradually less concentrated toward the bottom two-thirds of the cake.

STEP 3

Clean the spatula with a paper towel before swiping the next buttercream color onto the cake in the same random fashion, with the swipes of frosting more concentrated on the top and top third of the cake and less concentrated on the bottom two-thirds of the cake (C). When placing swipes directly next to other colors, try not to mix the colors together.

STEP 4

Repeat step 3 for each buttercream color in your palette until the top third of the cake looks completely filled with spatula-painted swipes and the bottom two-thirds look gradually less concentrated (D).

A

B

C

D

PAINTERLY

Buttercream makes the perfect medium for artistic techniques like this one, and the best part about this finish is that it's incredibly easy—you don't actually need art skills to make this finish look like a showstopper! This frosting finish is a great opportunity to showcase a pretty color palette and add intriguing texture to your cake. You can let the painterly finish shine as the main focus or use it as a backdrop for a drip (page 97) and other complementary decorations.

TOOLS & MATERIALS

1–2 cups (215–430 g) medium-consistency buttercream

Bowls and spoons for color mixing

Food coloring gels of your choice

A cake that's been frosted smooth (page 61) and chilled for at least 30 minutes

Turntable

Small icing spatula or palette knife

Icing smoother

TIPS FOR SUCCESS

Try to use three or four colors for the painted textures. These can be totally different hues or different shades of the same color (i.e., monochromatic).

If you aren't sure which colors to choose for your palette, reference the Color-Mixing Chart on page 57 for inspiration.

PAINTERLY TUTORIAL

STEP 1

Create your buttercream color palette. Divide the buttercream evenly between individual bowls and add food coloring gel to each bowl of frosting. Use a separate spoon to mix each color into the buttercream until you've created your desired color palette.

> **TIP:**
>
> For color-mixing instructions and inspiration, see "Your Guide to Coloring Buttercream" (pages 47–57).

STEP 2

With the chilled cake on the turn-table and starting with the first color in your palette, use a small icing spatula to randomly place swatches of buttercream, in varying sizes and shapes, onto the chilled cake (A). Then use an icing smoother to smooth down the swatches one by one (B). Repeat this step with at least one more color (C)—I typically create the smooth swatches with two colors and reserve the other colors for step 3.

STEP 3

Scoop ¼ to ½ teaspoon of colored buttercream onto a small icing spatula or palette knife, then swipe it onto the cake vertically to create a straight line (D). Repeat the vertical swiping motion directly next to the line you created to make a patch of vertical textured buttercream (E).

STEP 4

With the remaining colors in your palette, repeat step 3 wherever you'd like. This finish usually looks best with one or two different colors (F).

OMBRÉ

For the times you want to add depth to your color palette, an ombré finish is the way to go! It's easy, works in any color (even a chocolate ombré finish can look amazing) and can add a surreal element to your cake design. This tutorial will show you how to create a monochromatic ombré finish, which involves one color in three different shades. The ombré technique can also work with three completely different colors—just be sure to use colors that complement one another when they are mixed together.

TOOLS & MATERIALS

3 cups (645 g) medium-consistency buttercream

Bowls and spoons for color mixing

Food coloring gels of your choice

A cake that's been crumb coated (page 37) and chilled for at least 30 minutes

Turntable

Angled spatula

Icing smoother

TIPS FOR SUCCESS

When creating a monochromatic color palette, create the darkest color first. Then use the dark-colored buttercream to tint the other colors. This way, you keep all three colors in the palette true to the base color.

If you need color palette inspiration, take a look at the Color-Mixing Chart on page 57.

OMBRÉ TUTORIAL

STEP 1

Divide the buttercream between three bowls: Place about ¾ cup (161 g) in each of two bowls and place the remaining 1½ cups (323 g) in the third bowl. The bowl with the most buttercream will be for the top and top third of the cake.

In one of the bowls with ¾ cup (161 g) of buttercream, use food coloring gel and a spoon to mix the darkest color in your palette. Add the dark-colored buttercream, 2 teaspoons (8 g) at a time, to the bowl with 1½ cups (323 g) of buttercream to create the lightest color in your palette; alternatively, keep this bowl of butter-cream uncolored. Keep adding more dark buttercream or food coloring gel until you get the lightest shade to your liking. Then use the dark-colored buttercream or food coloring gel to create a shade that's between the light and dark shades.

STEP 2

With the crumb-coated and chilled cake on the turntable, use an angled spatula to apply the darkest buttercream to the bottom third of the cake (A). Next, apply the second-darkest buttercream to the middle third of the cake (B).

Add about ⅓ cup (72 g) of the lightest colored butter-cream in dollops to the top of the cake and smooth the frosting down with the angled spatula until it's about ¼ inch (6 mm) thick and reaches beyond the top edges of the cake. Then apply more light-colored buttercream to the top third of the cake (C).

TIP:

Don't worry about perfection when applying the buttercream colors to your cake. An uneven ombré gives the finish more dimension.

STEP 3

Using a clean angled spatula, gently make waves through the buttercream to blend the colors together where they meet (D).

STEP 4

Smooth the sides of the cake using the icing smoother according to steps 3 and 4 of the Smooth Buttercream Tutorial (page 62), filling any gaps along the way with the corresponding buttercream colors (E).

STEP 5

When the sides of the cake are smooth, turn the angled spatula 90 degrees and swipe the crown of buttercream inward, toward the center of the cake, to create sharp edges all around the top (F).

TEXTURED
BUTTERCREAM

Whenever I want to add intriguing texture to a cake without a lot of effort, I reach for either an icing comb or an icing spatula. Icing combs come in a variety of styles, each one designed to glide through frosting and create intricate textures that range from satisfying grooves to ornate designs. For more rustic textures, swiping an icing spatula through the buttercream will give you that unbridled look and feel. I recommend having both of these tools on hand for when you need a fast finish that looks high quality.

TOOLS & MATERIALS

A cake that's been crumb coated (page 37) and chilled for at least 30 minutes

Turntable

3 cups (645 g) medium-consistency buttercream

Icing smoother

Icing comb

Paper towels

Angled spatula

Icing spatula

TIPS FOR SUCCESS

Try to find stainless steel icing combs. They're much easier to clean and work with.

I use a 13-inch (33-cm) stainless steel angled spatula by Wilton to create symmetrical textures, but any size will do.

For rustic swirls, a smaller icing spatula (straight or angled) is my preference. I use a 9-inch (23-cm) straight spatula by Wilton.

These techniques look amazing in one color or combined with other techniques, like an ombré finish (page 77). Feel free to get creative with colors and textures!

COMB TEXTURE TUTORIAL

STEP 1

With the crumb-coated and chilled cake on the turn-table, complete steps 1 through 3 of the Smooth Buttercream Tutorial (page 62) using the buttercream and icing smoother, but don't worry about getting the top and sides super smooth. For this texture, you need only a semismooth finish that's about ½ inch (1.3 cm) thick (A).

STEP 2

Hold the icing comb next to the cake so that the icing comb is vertically straight and at a 45-degree angle to the sides of the cake. Place your free hand on the cake turntable directly in front of your cake and make a full rotation with the turntable as you let the icing comb gently glide through the frosting (B). Scrape any excess frosting from the icing comb and use a paper towel to wipe it clean.

STEP 3

Repeat step 2 until the grooves in the buttercream are as deep as you want them and the finish looks level and uniform (C). If you'd like to create sharp top edges instead of keeping them raw, swipe the buttercream crown on the top edge of the cake inward with an angled spatula (D).

TIP:

If you're having a hard time getting the frosting smooth in the places it needs to be, try heating up your icing comb by running it under hot water and drying it completely. Make sure it's just warm—not hot enough to easily melt the buttercream—before you comb the cake again.

A

B

C

D

SPATULA TEXTURE TUTORIALS

STEP 1

With the crumb-coated and chilled cake on the turntable, complete steps 1 through 3 of the Smooth Buttercream Tutorial (page 62) using the buttercream and icing smoother, but don't worry about getting the top and sides super smooth. For this texture, you need only a semismooth finish that's about ½ inch (1.3 cm) thick (A).

STEP 2

Use an angled spatula to create one of the following textures: symmetrical textures or rustic swirls.

SYMMETRICAL TEXTURES

Hold the angled spatula horizontally while you rotate the turntable to create grooves (B), swipe diagonally (C) or create vertical swipes (D).

Once you're finished with the texture on the side of the cake, feel free to get creative with the top! You can create the same texture on the top of the cake, leave it unfinished and rustic-looking, or swipe the excess buttercream inward to create a smooth top.

RUSTIC SWIRLS

Use an icing spatula to create swirls and swoops through the buttercream. Try some loose C and S shapes as you go along (E), as well as some quick swipes (F). You can't go wrong here, so don't be afraid to experiment with gentle swirls and more pronounced ones. Continue creating swirls on the sides and top of the cake until you're satisfied.

E

F

STRIPED
BUTTERCREAM

Perfectly symmetrical buttercream stripes on a cake are a thing of wonder. While you can certainly pipe the stripes onto the cake one by one, they won't be as symmetrical as if you were to use an icing comb (unless you've got the steadiest hands in the world, that is). You'll want to do this technique with an icing comb made specifically for creating striped buttercream. Then fill the grooves you create with a contrasting buttercream color and smooth it into an eye-catching striped masterpiece.

TOOLS & MATERIALS

4 cups (860 g) medium-consistency buttercream

Bowls and spoons for color mixing

Food coloring gels of your choice

A cake that's been frosted smooth (page 61) and chilled for at least 30 minutes

Turntable

Icing comb with square teeth

Paper towels

Angled spatula

Piping bag

Scissors

Icing smoother

TIPS FOR SUCCESS

Stainless steel icing combs are easier to work with and cleaner than plastic icing combs. Either kind will work for this tutorial. They come in a variety of sizes to create thinner or thicker stripes.

Use contrasting colors to make the stripes stand out.

Be patient with the smoothing process. It will look very messy before those perfect stripes appear.

STRIPED BUTTERCREAM TUTORIAL

If you plan on stripes that alternate between white and tinted buttercream, skip ahead to step 2 and tint only the buttercream that remains after step 4. This will ensure that your cake has alternating stripes of white and one other color.

If you plan on tinting both sets of stripes, so that the cake has two alternating colors, divide the 4 cups (860 g) of buttercream between two bowls: Place 3 cups (645 g) in the first bowl and 1 cup (215 g) in the second bowl. Use a spoon and food coloring gels to tint the 3 cups (645 g) of buttercream one color for the base stripes. Then tint the second bowl of buttercream a contrasting color for the alternating stripes.

STEP 2

Complete steps 1 through 3 of the Smooth Buttercream Tutorial (page 62) on the crumb-coated and chilled cake, but don't worry about getting the top and sides of the cake super smooth. For this cake, you need only a semismooth finish that's about ½ inch (1.3 cm) thick.

STEP 3

With the cake on the turntable, hold the icing comb next to the cake so that it's vertically straight and at a 90-degree angle to the cake's sides (A). Place your free hand on the turntable directly in front of the cake and make a full rotation with the turntable as you let the icing comb glide through the frosting and create grooves (B). Scrape any excess frosting on the icing comb onto the rim of the bowl that contains the corresponding color, and then use a paper towel to wipe the frosting comb clean.

STEP 4

Repeat step 3 until the grooves made with the icing comb are about as deep as the teeth cutouts on the icing comb (C). When you reach this point, swipe the top edges of the cake inward with an angled spatula to create sharp edges, and then refrigerate the cake for at least 30 minutes to let the frosting firm up. If you plan on stripes that alternate between white and tinted buttercream, tint the buttercream that is left over after you have completed this step.

STEP 5

Transfer the 1 cup (215 g) of tinted buttercream to a piping bag and use clean scissors to snip off a ¼-inch (6-mm) opening. Fill each of the frosting grooves with the buttercream in the piping bag (D). Make sure you pipe buttercream into each and every crevice and slightly overfill the grooves.

While filling the groves, hold your piping bag at different angles, so that you pipe buttercream into all the hard-to-reach places. This helps the stripes look uniform once you smooth them in step 6.

STEP 6

When every groove is filled with tinted buttercream, use one hand to hold an icing smoother next to the cake at the tightest possible angle while you rotate the turntable with your other hand. The frosting will look very messy before you start to see the stripes emerge (E). Wipe off your icing smoother with a paper towel after each rotation.

STEP 7

After several rotations, you will start to see those stripes emerging. Keep smoothing the cake with a gentle touch until it looks clean and uniform, then swipe the top edges inward to create sharp edges (F).

> **TIP:**
>
> If you're struggling with removing enough buttercream in some places, heat your icing smoother by running it under hot water, then dry it fully and wait until it's warm but not hot—otherwise it might melt the buttercream.

LAMBETH
PIPING

This style was made popular by Joseph Lambeth in the 1930s, and it is a fun vintage trend I can't get enough of. It makes any cake look a bit fancier and more retro chic. Lambeth piping basically combines symmetry with "overpiping," or creating rows of overlapping details with different piping tips. With this technique, more is definitely more, so feel free to stray from the tutorial and get even more creative with additional textures, colors and layers.

TOOLS & MATERIALS

4 piping bags

Wilton tips 6B, 4B, 32 and 104

3–4 cups (645–860 g) medium-consistency buttercream

Bowls and spoons for color mixing

Food coloring gels of your choice

A cake that's been frosted smooth (page 61) and chilled for at least 30 minutes

Round cake board with a diameter at least 1 inch (2.5 cm) larger than the cake

Turntable

Round cake pan that is the same diameter as the cake

Wax or parchment paper

Pencil

Scissors

Toothpick

Circular cookie cutter or glass

Scotch® tape

TIPS FOR SUCCESS

Use a medium- to stiff-consistency buttercream for all of the piped elements.

Practice piping on a baking sheet or other flat surface to get the hang of it before you start piping on the cake.

Refer to pages 109 to 117 for more information on piping tips and techniques.

LAMBETH PIPING TUTORIAL

STEP 1

Fit each of the piping bags with each of the four tips (see page 110 for a tutorial on preparing piping bags). Divide the buttercream evenly between four bowls and, using spoons and food coloring gels, tint each portion of buttercream to your liking. Fill each prepared piping bag with a different color of buttercream.

STEP 2

Transfer the chilled smooth buttercream cake to the larger cake board (see page 118 for a tutorial on how to transfer successfully). Transfer the cake board to the turntable.

Place the cake pan on top of the wax paper and trace around the pan with a pencil before cutting out the circle with scissors. Fold the circle in half three times to form eight creases (A). Unfold the circle and place it on top of the cake. Anywhere there is a crease, create a mark with a toothpick on the side of the cake (B), then remove the paper template. This will help you divide the cake into eight equal sections for perfect piping all the way around.

STEP 3

Find a large circular cookie cutter or glass that's the same diameter as the space between each toothpick mark you created in step 2. Place a piece of Scotch tape across the cutter to help you line it up with the top edge of the cake (C). Using the toothpick marks as your guide, gently press the cookie cutter into the sides of the cake to create eight half circles (D).

STEP 4

Using a Wilton tip 6B, pipe a shell border (page 116) along the bottom edge of the cake, then pipe a shell border with the same tip along the top edge of the cake (E). Using a Wilton tip 32, pipe an even smaller shell border directly above the border on the bottom of the cake and inside the shell border on top of the cake (F).

STEP 5

Leaving about ½ inch (1.3 cm) of space between the top of the cake and where you begin and end each garland, pipe a ruffle (page 114) along each half circle to make a ruffled garland using a Wilton tip 104 (G). Pipe a large vertical shell using a Wilton tip 4B where each garland connects (H).

STEP 6

Use a Wilton tip 32 to pipe two small overlapping shells beneath each garland as pictured (I).

A   B   C   D   E   F   G   H   I

FINISHING
TOUCHES

No matter what kind of frosting finish you use to decorate a cake, there are always more opportunities to get creative with the rest of the details. These next few pages will walk you through all of my favorite ways to add extra intrigue to cake designs, from glistening ganache drips to pretty sprinkles, piped textures, buttercream borders and everything in between. Feel free to keep things simple with just a few of these finishing touches or mix and match several of them—when it comes to cake design, more is more!

GANACHE DRIP CAKES

Whether you're working with Chocolate Ganache Drip (page 135) or White Chocolate Ganache Drip (page 136), these methods and techniques for creating a drip cake will be the same.

TIPS FOR SUCCESS

Be patient with the cooling process. Once you've whisked the ganache together, it's crucial to let it cool on your counter for 10 to 20 minutes, until it's room temperature or slightly warmer. Trying to speed up this process by placing the ganache in the refrigerator doesn't usually end well—I've found that it cools unevenly, leading to thick, globby drips.

Don't overstir. Ganache, especially white chocolate ganache, does not like to be stirred too often. Be sure to stir only when you're checking the consistency, which will likely be every 5 to 10 minutes until the drip consistency is reached. If you end up overstirring, the ganache may start to look dull and grainy or separated. Page 103 provides trouble-shooting tips for what to do if this happens.

Start with a chilled buttercream cake. There's a science to this tip. Since molecules move more slowly at cooler temperatures, it makes sense that you can better control how far the drips travel when the buttercream is chilled. Make sure that, after you apply your final coat of buttercream, you chill the cake in the refrigerator for at least 30 minutes.

Practice makes perfect. As with all elements of cake decorating, you will get better and better the more you practice your ganache drips and follow along with this guide. It can be very intimidating to drip a cake, but I promise that, with time, you will be able to tell when the ganache consistency is perfect and control the drips so that they end up exactly where you want them.

HOW TO DRIP A CAKE

Start with a test drip. After your ganache has been made and you've allowed it to cool to room temperature or slightly above, it can be very helpful to test the consistency before you commit to dripping your cake. You can do this by gently nudging the ganache off the top edge of a tall glass with a spoon. Allow the ganache to run down the side.

If the test drip travels rapidly and pools at the bottom of the glass, your ganache is too warm (A). Allow the ganache to cool for another 5 to 10 minutes before trying your test drip again.

If the test drip is gloppy or doesn't travel very far down the side of the glass, it's too cold (B). To fix the consistency, reheat the ganache in the microwave for about 10 seconds, stir it and try again. Repeat the reheating process as needed until you get the perfect consistency.

If the test drip travels about halfway down the glass and stops, you're ready to create a traditional drip or a curtain drip (C).

TIP:

If you start a drip on your cake and find it's not coming out right, you can still save it! To remove a drip from your cake, place the cake in the refrigerator for 5 to 10 minutes to let the ganache firm up, then gently scrape it off with a spatula and try again.

TOO WARM AND RUNNY

A

TOO COLD AND THICK

B

JUST RIGHT!

C

TRADITIONAL DRIP TUTORIAL

When you think of drip cakes, the traditional drip is most likely what you're imagining. This technique allows you to place the drips where you want them on your cake. As long as your ganache consistency is just right, you'll even be able to control how long or short you want them to be.

STEP 1

You can complete this step with either a spoon or a piping bag.

To use a spoon, carefully nudge spoonfuls of ganache over the top edges of the cake (A). Nudge larger spoonfuls of ganache for longer drips and smaller spoonfuls for shorter ones.

To use a piping bag, fill a piping bag with ganache before snipping off a ⅛-inch (3-mm) opening on the end. Then hold the piping bag over the top edge of the cake and gently squeeze the piping bag to release ganache over the edge (B). The more tightly you squeeze the piping bag, the longer the drips will be.

Continue creating drips over the top edges of the cake with either a spoon or piping bag until you've gone around the entire cake (C).

STEP 2

Place 2 to 3 tablespoons (30 to 45 ml) of ganache on the very top of the cake (D) and spread it with an angled spatula just until it fills the empty spaces (E). It should self-level a bit, so don't worry too much about getting it super smooth.

STEP 3

Pop the cake into the refrigerator for at least 5 minutes to let the ganache set up before moving on with your decorating.

HALF DRIP VARIATION

This is the same technique you'd use with the traditional drip, but instead of creating drips around the entire cake, you'll stop at the halfway point. I love pairing this look with a crescent buttercream border (page 116) for an elegant design (F).

CURTAIN DRIP TUTORIAL

This technique is a bit more rustic and unbridled than the traditional drip. Instead of controlling where the ganache drips will go, you'll essentially be pouring ganache over the top of the cake and letting the drips fall where they may. Your cake will look like it is draped in a curtain of dripping ganache, hence the name.

STEP 1

Place your cold buttercream cake on a turntable. Pour about ½ cup (120 ml) of ganache on the top of the cake (A).

STEP 2

Rotate the turntable with your free hand while you smooth the ganache down with an angled spatula to move it toward the cake's edges (B). Continue gently smoothing and rotating until the ganache starts to blanket the sides of the cake, then let the drips fall where they may (C).

A

B

C

GANACHE TROUBLESHOOTING

The more you practice, the easier it will be to recognize when the ganache is the perfect consistency for creating a drip cake. Still, there may be times when you need to troubleshoot or even rescue your ganache if things go sideways. The following table outlines the most common problems that can happen with ganache and how to solve them.

TROUBLESHOOTING GANACHE

Problem	Cause	Solution
The ganache is too runny at room temperature.	If you've let the ganache cool for a significant amount of time and the drips are still too runny, it means that too much liquid (heavy whipping cream, icing whitener or color gel) was incorporated into the recipe.	Thicken the ganache with more chocolate. Melt an additional 1 to 2 ounces (28 to 56 g) of chocolate in the microwave, warm the existing ganache to the same temperature as the melted chocolate and then whisk it all together before letting it cool down to the ideal drip consistency.
The drips are thick and gloppy.	This usually means your ganache is too set, or too cold, to create drips.	Gently warm the ganache in the microwave in 5- to 10-second increments until it becomes the ideal drip consistency.
The ganache is too thick, even when it is warm.	This means that you may need to add a little more liquid to thin the ganache.	Add 1 to 2 teaspoons (5 to 10 ml) of heavy cream to the ganache, then microwave it for 10 to 15 seconds and whisk it all together. Let the ganache cool to room temperature before trying the test drip again. Repeat the process of adding more cream until the consistency is ideal.
The ganache has split.	If your ganache looks grainy or seized, it means that the fat is separating from the liquid.	Gently reheat the ganache in the microwave or over a double boiler to 92°F (33°C) to melt the fat crystals, then whisk the ganache to bring it back together.

ADDING
SPRINKLES

There are several techniques for adding sprinkles to a cake, and the following are a few of my go-tos. You can combine all three techniques to create an ombré-sprinkle look, like the cake on the cover of this book, or you can pick and choose which ones to use. They look great alone or combined.

TIPS FOR SUCCESS

Use high-quality sprinkles for best results. My favorite brands to use are Sprinkle Pop and Fancy Sprinkles. You may also be able to find some quality sprinkle options at your local craft store or on Amazon.

These sprinkle techniques work best on cakes that have just been frosted, meaning the buttercream is still slightly sticky for the sprinkles to adhere.

A

SPRINKLE BORDER

STEP 1

Place a large baking sheet underneath your cake turntable. This helps catch any sprinkles that fall off the cake, saving you from having to break out the broom afterward.

STEP 2

Pour the sprinkles into the palm of your hand (A), then gently press them onto the bottom third of the cake (B). This is easiest when the cake has just been frosted and the buttercream is still slightly sticky.

STEP 3

Rotate the turntable as you repeat step 2 all around the bottom third of the cake (C). Don't worry about keeping the border even—it looks better with some highs and lows. When you're finished, brush the excess sprinkles off the turntable.

B

C

FLOATING SPRINKLES

STEP 1

Pour about ¼ cup (50 g) of sprinkles onto a flat surface. Then press the pad of your pointer finger onto a sprinkle until it sticks when you lift your finger (A).

If you're having a hard time getting the sprinkles to stick to your finger, try pressing your finger to a moist cloth first to make your skin a little tackier.

STEP 2

Using the pad of your finger, carefully press the sprinkle to the side of the cake (B). If the sprinkles are too large to stick to the pad of your finger, you should be able to pinch them between your thumb and pointer finger then gently place them on the side of the cake. Placing sprinkles either way is easiest when the cake has just been frosted and the buttercream is still slightly sticky.

STEP 3

Repeat steps 1 and 2, placing the sprinkles 1 to 2 inches (2.5 to 5 cm) apart around the entire cake.

> TIP:
>
> If you want to create more of an ombré look, place the sprinkles closer together toward the bottom third of the cake and farther apart as you reach the top third.

A

B

SPRINKLE GARNISHES

Grab a pinch of sprinkles and slowly release them a few at a time as you hover your hand over the cake (C). This works best when the buttercream border has just been piped and the buttercream is still slightly sticky, so that the sprinkles adhere well.

C

BUTTERCREAM
PIPING

Piping with buttercream is one of my favorite ways to add details and finishing touches to cakes. Whether you're going for some simple swirls on top or a more intricate buttercream border, piping can help round out the cake design with intriguing textures. Feel free to pair the following techniques with a colorful buttercream palette (page 54), or stick to whatever color your buttercream is naturally.

TIPS FOR SUCCESS

To make sure your piping is perfectly detailed, use either medium-consistency or stiff-consistency buttercream (page 44). Buttercream that is too thin or soft will not hold its shape when piped.

A Wilton tip 1M and a Wilton tip 4B are the perfect tips to start your piping tip collection, as they are the most versatile, in my opinion. If you need more recommendations on which piping tips to add to your collection, page 112 shows my favorites.

HOW TO PREPARE A PIPING BAG

STEP 1

With a clean pair of scissors, snip off a ¼- to ½-inch (6-mm to 1.3-cm) opening at the pointed end of the piping bag. (The size of the opening depends on how small or large the piping tip is.) Then place a piping tip inside the bag (A). You'll want to make sure the opening you create is just wide enough for the decorative edges of the tip to peek out, yet small enough to hold the tip in place when you pipe with it.

STEP 2

Place the piping bag, tip down, into a tall glass and fold the edges of the bag over the rim of the glass (B). Scoop buttercream into the bag using a rubber spatula or spoon (C).

STEP 3

Unfold the edges of the piping bag from the rim of the glass and twist the unfilled end of the piping bag to close it off, pushing the buttercream down toward the piping tip in the process (D). Now you're ready to pipe away!

PIPING BAG TIPS

Make sure that any grooves in your piping tip are fully exposed and not covered by any part of the bag before you start filling it with buttercream. If there is any overhang from the bag, simply remove the piping tip and cut a slightly larger opening before reinserting the piping tip.

Fill your piping bag no more than ⅔ full. Otherwise, the bag will most likely overflow when you squeeze it, which could make for an unpleasant piping session.

After you prepare your piping bag, position the end of the bag in the palm of your dominant hand while pinching the twisted end between your thumb and pointer finger. Position your other hand near the tip as support. Squeeze the contents of the bag from the base (twisted portion) down.

Remember that perfect piping takes practice! If you don't feel ready to pipe directly onto your cake, practice on a cookie sheet or other flat surface to get the hang of it first.

A

B

C

D

MY FAVORITE PIPING TIPS

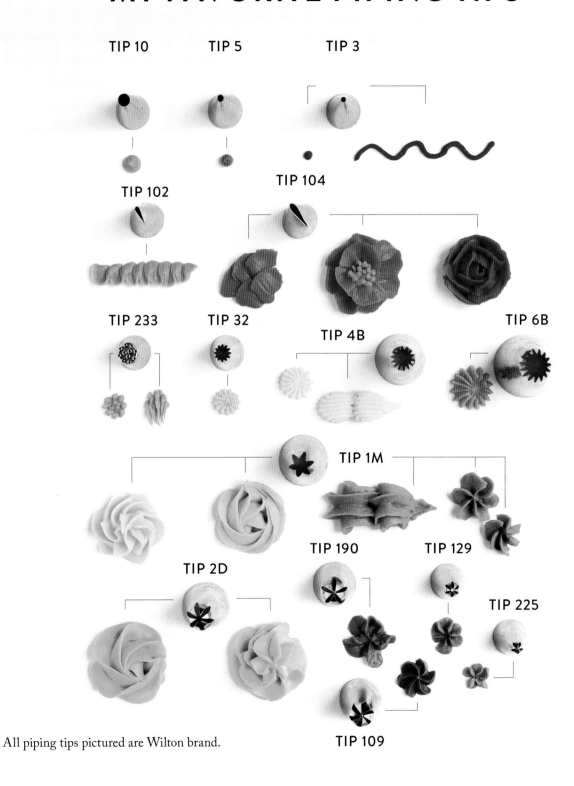

TIP 10   TIP 5   TIP 3

TIP 102   TIP 104

TIP 233   TIP 32   TIP 4B   TIP 6B

TIP 1M   TIP 190   TIP 129

TIP 2D   TIP 225

TIP 109

All piping tips pictured are Wilton brand.

A　　　　　　　　B　　　　　　　　C

HOW TO PIPE BASIC SHAPES

STARS (PICTURED ABOVE)

This is one of my favorite shapes, because the piping tip truly does all the work for you. To pipe a star, fit a piping bag with a star tip (Wilton tips 4B, 6B and 16 work great). Hold the piping bag straight with the piping tip at a 90-degree angle, hovering about ¼ inch (6 mm) above the surface of the cake (A). Squeeze the piping bag until the buttercream makes contact with the cake's surface and begins to spread out slightly (B), then pull up as you release pressure (C).

ROSETTES (PICTURED BELOW)

These are among the easiest floral accents you can add to your cakes. To create a rosette, fit a piping bag with a star tip—Wilton tips 1M, 2D and 4B are some of my favorites. Hold the piping bag straight with the piping tip at a 90-degree angle to the cake's surface. Squeeze the bag to form a star (A), then—without releasing pressure—raise the tip slightly and move it to one side of the star before moving it in a circular motion tightly around the star (B). Decrease the pressure on the piping bag as you approach one full rotation around the star (C).

A　　　　　　　　B　　　　　　　　C

A	B	C

RUFFLES (PICTURED ABOVE)

Knowing how to pipe the perfect buttercream ruffle comes in handy whenever you want to add some extra frills to a cake. Fit a piping bag with a Wilton tip 104. Hold the piping bag at a 45-degree angle to the surface of the cake with the skinny end of the tip facing away from the cake (A). Squeeze the piping bag as you move your hand slightly up and down to create the ruffle texture as you pipe (B). Release pressure on the piping bag once you've ended the ruffle where you desire (C).

SHELLS (PICTURED BELOW)

This shape is perfect for creating borders on your cake for a vintage look or for adding unique textured accents. To create a shell, fit a piping bag with a star tip like a Wilton tip 4B, 6B or 16. Hold the piping bag at a 45-degree angle (A) and squeeze hard until the buttercream fans out and forces the tip upward (B). Gradually relax pressure as you lower the piping tip and pull the piping bag toward you to create a tail (C).

A	B	C

These are some of the most common shapes for creating borders and topping cupcakes. This technique works with many different piping tip shapes, but my favorites to use are Wilton tips 1M, 4B and 2D.

To create a swirl, prepare a piping bag with your desired tip. Hold the piping bag straight up, with the piping tip at a 90-degree angle to the cake's surface. Squeeze the bag as you rotate your hand in a circular motion (A).

A

When you approach one full rotation, continue applying pressure to the bag as you pipe another slightly smaller circle of buttercream directly on top of the first (B).

Continue overlapping with smaller circles until they come to a point, then release pressure (C).

B

C

BUTTERCREAM BORDERS

ROPE BORDER (A)

Prepare a piping bag with a large piping tip—Wilton tips 1M, 4B or 6B are great choices. Hold the piping bag at a 45-degree angle on the top edge of the cake, about ½ inch (1.3 cm) inward, then pipe a clockwise circle. Continue piping overlapping circles in the same clockwise motion, keeping the piping bag at a 45-degree angle, all along the edge of the cake until you reach the first circle you created.

BRAIDED BORDER (B)

Prepare a piping bag with a Wilton tip 1M or 4B. Hold the piping bag at a 45-degree angle and pipe a diagonal line, starting at the outer edge and ending about ½ inch (1.3 cm) inward. Pipe another diagonal line next to the first, going in the opposite direction, so that the second line overlaps the first to make a V shape. Repeat the overlapping Vs all around the top edge of the cake.

SWIRLS (C)

Prepare a piping bag with a large piping tip—Wilton tips 1M, 4B or 2D are great choices. Pipe swirls (page 115) directly next to one another all around the top of the cake. To make the swirls perfectly spaced, you can pipe one swirl as a starting point then pipe another directly across from it. Pipe an equal number of swirls between each of those first two.

STARS (D)

Prepare a piping bag with a large star tip, such as a Wilton 6B or 8B. Hold the piping bag at a 90-degree angle on the top edge of the cake with the piping tip about ½ inch (1.3 cm) from the cake's surface. Squeeze the piping bag to create a star shape, and once the buttercream touches the surface of the cake and begins to spread, pull up on the bag while releasing pressure. Repeat this process, placing the stars directly next to each other all along the top edge.

CRESCENT BORDER (E)

Prepare one piping bag with a Wilton tip 1M, one with a Wilton tip 4B and one with a Wilton tip 16. Pipe rosettes (page 113) and stars (page 113) in a crescent shape on half of the top of the cake.

SHELL BORDER (F)

Prepare a piping bag with a Wilton tip 6B or another large star tip. Hold the piping bag at a 45-degree angle and pipe a shell (page 114), then pipe another shell onto the tail of the previous one. Repeat this process, each shell overlapping, until you connect with the first shell you piped.

HOW TO TRANSFER A CAKE

Now that you've got a beautiful layer cake—complete with finishing touches—before you on the turntable, you might be feeling the panic set in as you wonder how to move the cake to a stand or a box. Sure, you can always decorate the cake on a larger cake board (see Tip), but if you want the cake to look seamless on a cake stand, here's how to do it.

STEP 1

Chill the cake on the turntable until the frosting is firm to the touch. Heat a paring knife under hot water and dry it completely, then run it all along the bottom edge of the cake to separate it from the turntable (A).

STEP 2

Slide an angled spatula underneath the cake and lift the edge up high enough to slide one hand underneath (B).

STEP 3

Use your free hand to support the top or side of the cake while you transfer it to the stand (C). I know it seems risky, but the frosting should be cold enough for you to handle it without indenting it or otherwise messing it up.

A

B

C

> **TIP:**
>
> If you'd rather decorate your cake on a larger cake board to make the transfer process even easier, go for it! Use either a cardboard or acrylic cake circle that's at least 1 inch (2.5 cm) larger in diameter than the cake. When you're done decorating, simply lift the cake board and transfer it to a stand or box.

DECORATING FAQS & TROUBLESHOOTING GUIDE

Cake decorating lets you have fun and lets your creativity shine. There are also quite a few learning curves that come along with decorating, and nobody that I know of has ever started their cake decorating journey making flawless cakes. Let's prevent potential failure: In the following paragraphs, you'll find my collection of troubleshooting tips for the most common cake decorating issues I've experienced, plus answers to the most frequently asked questions on my blog regarding this topic.

How much buttercream do I need?

This depends on many factors: the size of your cake, the style of frosting finish you're going for, whether you're planning on using buttercream as filling between layers and whether you'll be piping decorations with it (to name a few). I will say that it's always better to have a little more buttercream than you expected than to not have enough. To prevent that scenario, always round up when estimating buttercream amounts.

Each buttercream recipe in Chapter 4 (page 123) yields about 3 cups (645 g) of buttercream. With that in mind, the following are two helpful charts to reference for your estimations based on the cake sizes and decorations in this book.

BUTTERCREAM AMOUNTS FOR CAKES

Size of Cake	Number of Layers	Filling and Crumb Coat	Frosting	Total
6 inches (15 cm)	2	1½ cups (323 g)	1½ cups (323 g)	3 cups (646 g)
6 inches (15 cm)	3	2½ cups (538 g)	2½ cups (538 g)	5 cups (1.1 kg)
8 inches (20 cm)	2	2 cups (430 g)	2½ cups (538 g)	4½ cups (968 g)
8 inches (20 cm)	3	3 cups (645 g)	3 cups (645 g)	6 cups (1.3 kg)

BUTTERCREAM AMOUNTS FOR BORDERS

Border Design	Total Amount of Buttercream
Star border	1 cup (215 g)
Swirl border	1½ cups (323 g)
Braided border	1½ cups (323 g)
Rope border	2 cups (430 g)
Shell border	1½ cups (323 g)
Crescent border	1½ cups (323 g)

Why does my buttercream look curdled?

The two most common reasons buttercream might curdle are (1) using butter that is too soft and (2) adding milk that is too cold. Both of these ingredients must be at room temperature for the buttercream to have a cohesive, smooth consistency. To fix it, place the entire batch of buttercream in the refrigerator for about 20 minutes, then remix it with your stand mixer for 2 to 3 minutes. It should look well blended and smooth at this point.

Why is my buttercream grainy?

Grainy buttercream is usually the result of either not sifting large lumps out of the powdered sugar or not mixing the buttercream long enough. To fix the consistency, add 1 to 2 teaspoons (5 to 10 ml) of room-temperature milk and mix the buttercream at low speed for 1 to 2 minutes. This will help the powdered sugar dissolve and eliminate the graininess.

Why are there air bubbles in my buttercream and how do I get rid of them?

If you're seeing air bubbles in your buttercream right after you've mixed it up, it means you've incorporated too much air into it. Place it in an airtight container and let it rest for 20 to 30 minutes, then transfer it back to the stand mixer and mix it at the lowest speed for 1 to 2 minutes. This should push all of the extra air out and leave you with super smooth buttercream.

If you didn't notice the air bubbles until you started frosting your cake, fear not. Finish frosting a very thin coat of buttercream on your cake (air bubbles and all), then place the cake in the refrigerator while you fix the rest of the buttercream as detailed in the preceding paragraph. Once your batch of buttercream is rid of air bubbles, you can continue frosting the cake. The additional layer of buttercream will fill in and cover any air bubbles as you frost.

Why did an air bubble suddenly appear on my finished cake?

If you're seeing an air bubble on your cake after frosting and decorating it, that usually means that the final coating of buttercream didn't properly adhere to the crumb coat layer and there is a pocket of air trapped inside. That pocket of air is trying to escape, thus creating an unsightly air bubble.

To get rid of an air bubble, you can pop it with a clean toothpick. Then gently press down on the area with a metal spatula to flatten the frosting. To help prevent air bubbles next time, be sure to firmly press the buttercream onto the cake when applying it, so that every square inch of the crumb coat is covered with an even layer of buttercream. You may also consider piping the buttercream onto your cake to ensure an even layer, as opposed to applying it with a spatula, before continuing on with your frosting finish.

How do I fix buttercream that's too thin or too thick?

See the section titled "Buttercream Frosting Consistency" on page 44.

Where can I find quality food coloring gels?

Try your local craft store, cake decorating shop or online resources like Amazon. My favorite products to use are AmeriColor Soft Gel Paste and the Wilton Color Right Performance Color System.

What should I do if the buttercream in my piping bag starts to get too soft?

This can happen due to heat, either from overhandling the piping bag with warm hands or from a warm kitchen environment. To fix it, place the filled piping bag in the refrigerator for 10 to 15 minutes. Next, gently knead the buttercream inside the piping bag to create a cohesive consistency. At this point, it will be ready to reuse.

Do I have to use American buttercream with these tutorials and techniques?

Any kind of buttercream or frosting that you'd normally use to decorate a cake will work. Some may be more difficult to color than American buttercream—but other than that issue, you should be able to pair your preferred type of buttercream with any technique and tutorial in this book.

What kind of buttercream should I make for hot weather?

Buttercream starts to soften when the temperature is 75°F (24°C) and above, and it can fully melt if placed in direct sunlight. To make any of my buttercream recipes more heat resistant, substitute half of the butter in the recipe with high-ratio shortening and add 1 tablespoon (10 g) of meringue powder per batch of buttercream. This will stabilize the buttercream and make it much less prone to melt in hot weather.

Chapter 4
ESSENTIAL RECIPES

I am a firm believer that everyone who loves cake should have at least one go-to cake recipe. These are the recipes you reach for when you need to whip up a birthday cake at the last minute or make a quick batch of buttercream to practice your piping skills. It could be your grandma's chocolate cake recipe, that salted caramel recipe that gets all the compliments, the first successful buttercream you ever made—whatever the story, it's important to find those favorite recipes you can stick in your recipe box and hand down to future generations.

In this chapter, you'll find my collection of go-to cake recipes that have been tried and tested for many years. I've made them so many times that I have them memorized. From the chocolate ganache I use for all my drip cakes to the vanilla cake recipe I refined until it was absolutely perfect, these are the essentials I have come to depend on. My hope is that you find them so marvelous and dependable that they end up in your recipe box for good.

One-Bowl Chocolate Cake

Yield: 6 cups (1.4 L) batter; 3 (6-inch [15-cm]) layers or 2 (8-inch [20-cm]) layers
Prep time: 15 minutes   **Bake time:** 32–36 minutes

My love for chocolate runs deep. Therefore, I have extremely high standards for chocolate cake. It must be moist and fudgy, rich and decadent, nostalgic—basically, the kind of cake you could eat any time of the day because it always sounds satisfying. This chocolate cake recipe is all of the above yet easy to whip up using one bowl and some simple ingredients. I like to use hot coffee in this recipe because it does a great job of amplifying the chocolate flavor, but you can substitute coffee with hot water and still have a delicious chocolate cake. Pair this cake with Chocolate Buttercream (page 132) to make the ultimate chocolate cake, or use your imagination when it comes to fillings and frostings—this cake goes with anything!

2 cups (266 g) all-purpose flour

1⅔ cups (332 g) granulated sugar

⅔ cup (60 g) unsweetened natural cocoa powder

2 tsp (10 g) baking soda

1 tsp baking powder

½ tsp salt

½ cup (120 ml) vegetable oil

2 large eggs, at room temperature

1½ tsp (8 ml) pure vanilla extract

1 cup (240 ml) full-fat buttermilk, at room temperature

1 cup (240 ml) hot coffee or hot water

1. Preheat the oven to 350°F (177°C) and prepare three 6-inch (15-cm) or two 8-inch (20-cm) round cake pans by spraying the sides with baking spray and fitting a parchment paper circle to the bottom of each pan.

2. In the bowl of a stand mixer fitted with the paddle attachment, combine the flour, sugar, cocoa powder, baking soda, baking powder and salt. Stir the ingredients together at low speed for 30 seconds to fully combine them. Add the oil, eggs, vanilla and buttermilk and mix the ingredients at low speed until just combined. With the mixer still running at low speed, add the coffee or water in a slow stream. Mix the batter at low speed for 1 to 2 minutes, until the ingredients are fully combined and the batter is smooth. The batter will be very thin.

3. Divide the batter evenly between the prepared cake pans. Bake the cakes for 32 to 36 minutes, until a wooden toothpick inserted into the centers comes out clean. Allow the cakes to cool completely before frosting them.

Favorite Vanilla Cake

Yield: 6 cups (1.4 L) batter; 3 (6-inch [15-cm]) layers or 2 (8-inch [20-cm]) layers
Prep time: 25 minutes   **Bake time:** 30–35 minutes

One of the very first cake recipes I wrote from scratch was this vanilla cake. It sounds plain and simple, but let me tell you that developing this recipe felt like summiting a mountain. The trouble was that I'd become accustomed to the fluffy yet moist texture of boxed cake mixes and just couldn't seem to replicate that with from-scratch recipes. So, I tested what felt like hundreds of recipes in search of the perfect vanilla cake. The moment I cut into this one, I was so overcome by its texture that I jumped around the kitchen with glee. It's soft and moist, packed with vanilla flavor and pairs well with many frosting and filling combinations. It's been a blog-reader favorite since I posted it years ago, and I love it so much that I've used it as the starting point for many other cake recipes—it's that versatile!

2¾ cups (292 g) sifted cake flour

2 tsp (10 g) baking powder

½ tsp baking soda

1 tsp salt

¾ cup (170 g) unsalted butter, at room temperature

1½ cups (300 g) granulated sugar

2 large eggs plus 2 large egg whites, at room temperature

1 tbsp (15 ml) pure vanilla extract

½ cup (120 g) sour cream, at room temperature

1 cup (240 ml) whole milk, at room temperature

1. Preheat the oven to 350°F (177°C). Prepare three 6-inch (15-cm) or two 8-inch (20-cm) round cake pans by spraying the sides with baking spray and fitting a parchment paper circle to the bottom of each pan.

2. Place the flour, baking powder, baking soda and salt in a medium bowl and whisk the ingredients to combine them. Set the flour mixture aside.

3. In the bowl of a stand mixer fitted with the paddle attachment, beat the butter at high speed for about 2 minutes, until it is creamy. Add the sugar and mix the ingredients at medium-high speed for 2 minutes, scraping the bowl and paddle at the halfway point. Decrease the mixer's speed to low and add the eggs and egg whites, one at a time, mixing until they are just combined and scraping the bowl and paddle as needed. Add the vanilla and sour cream, increase the mixer's speed to high and beat the ingredients for 1 minute. The mixture will look curdled at this point, but don't worry—it will become smooth at the end.

4. Turn the mixer off and add the flour mixture all at once. Start the mixer at low speed. Mix until the ingredients are just combined, and then, with the mixer still running, slowly pour in the milk. Mix the ingredients at low speed for about 30 seconds, until they are just combined. Scrape the sides and bottom of the bowl and stir the batter with a whisk a few times to make sure there are no lumps. The batter will be slightly thick.

5. Divide the batter evenly between the prepared cake pans. Bake the cakes for 30 to 35 minutes. The cakes are done when they spring back to the touch and a toothpick inserted into the centers comes out clean. Let the cakes cool in their pans for 5 minutes, and then remove them from the pans and allow them to cool on a wire rack for a few hours. Make sure the cakes are entirely at room temperature before applying frosting.

Bakery-Style White Cake

Yield: 6 cups (1.4 L) batter; 3 (6-inch [15-cm]) layers or 2 (8-inch [20-cm]) layers
Prep time: 25 minutes   **Bake time:** 28–32 minutes

With its melt-in-your-mouth texture and the perfect vanilla flavor, this cake seems to come straight from a great bakery's top-secret recipe box. It's called a white cake because it uses only egg whites—without yolks to saturate the batter, the resulting cake is white in color. The egg whites are also responsible for making the cake fluffy, while cake flour gives it a super soft crumb. Buttermilk and vegetable oil add the perfect amount of moisture. I love this recipe so much that I use it as a base for other recipes, like my Raspberry-Almond Impressionist Cake (page 187) and Lemon-Raspberry Painterly Cake (page 180).

2½ cups (265 g) sifted cake flour

2 tsp (10 g) baking powder

½ tsp baking soda

½ tsp salt

½ cup (113 g) unsalted butter, at room temperature

1½ cups (300 g) granulated sugar

4 large egg whites, at room temperature

½ cup (120 ml) vegetable oil

1 tbsp (15 ml) pure vanilla extract

1¼ cups (300 ml) full-fat buttermilk, at room temperature

1. Preheat the oven to 350°F (177°C). Prepare three 6-inch (15-cm) or two 8-inch (20-cm) round cake pans by spraying the sides with baking spray and fitting a parchment paper circle to the bottom of each pan.

2. In a medium bowl, combine the flour, baking powder, baking soda and salt. Whisk the ingredients to combine them, and then set the bowl aside.

3. In the bowl of a stand mixer fitted with the paddle attachment, beat the butter at high speed for about 2 minutes, until it is creamy. Add the sugar and mix the ingredients at medium-high speed for 2 minutes, scraping the bowl and paddle at the halfway point. Decrease the mixer's speed to low and add the egg whites, one at a time, mixing until they are just combined and scraping the bowl and paddle as needed. Add the vegetable oil and vanilla, increase the mixer's speed to high and beat the ingredients for 1 minute.

4. Turn the mixer off and add the flour mixture all at once. Start the mixer at low speed. Mix until the ingredients are just combined, and then, with the mixer still running, slowly pour in the buttermilk. Mix the ingredients at low speed for about 30 seconds, until they are just combined. Scrape the sides and bottom of the bowl and stir the batter with a whisk a few times to make sure there are no lumps.

5. Divide the batter evenly between the prepared cake pans. Bake the cakes for 28 to 32 minutes. They're done when they spring back to the touch and a toothpick inserted into the centers comes out clean or with just a few moist crumbs on it. Let the cakes cool in their pans for 5 minutes, then remove them from the pans and allow them to cool completely on a wire rack.

Cream Cheese Buttercream

Yield: 3 cups (650 g)   **Prep time:** 20 minutes

When I ran a home bakery business years ago, cream cheese buttercream was one of my most requested frosting flavors. I used to dread working with it because it's much softer than your average American buttercream. But over the years, I tweaked the recipe to be a bit more stable for filling, frosting and even piping decorations! Now it's a joy to work with. This buttercream is delicious, borderline addicting and makes any cake all the more decadent. My favorite recipes to pair it with are the Vintage Piped Red Velvet Cake (page 163), Semi-Naked Carrot Cake (page 194), Lemon-Raspberry Painterly Cake (page 180) and One-Bowl Chocolate Cake (page 125).

4 cups (480 g) powdered sugar

¼ cup (32 g) cornstarch (optional; see Notes)

½ cup (113 g) unsalted butter, at room temperature

8 oz (224 g) full-fat cream cheese, at room temperature (see Notes)

1½ tsp (8 ml) pure vanilla extract

¼ tsp salt

1. Sift together the powdered sugar and cornstarch (if using) in a medium bowl. Set the bowl aside.

2. In the bowl of a stand mixer fitted with the paddle attachment, cream together the butter and cream cheese at high speed for about 5 minutes, until the mixture is light, fluffy and uniform with no lumps. Decrease the mixer's speed to low and add the powdered sugar–cornstarch mixture, 1 cup (240 g) at a time, mixing thoroughly after each addition. Add the vanilla and salt and mix the frosting for 1 minute, until the ingredients are fully combined and the frosting is smooth.

TIP:

In addition to cornstarch, you can thicken the consistency of this buttercream by popping it into the refrigerator for 10 to 15 minutes to let the butter in the recipe firm up slightly. Then mix it at low speed for 1 minute. This should make the buttercream easier to work with for filling, frosting and piping.

NOTES

Cornstarch helps thicken the consistency of the Cream Cheese Buttercream without adding any flavor. I highly recommend it if you're using this frosting to pipe intricate details (such as on the Vintage Piped Red Velvet Cake on page 163).

Use brick-style cream cheese in this recipe, not the spreadable kind. The latter has too much liquid content to make a stable frosting.

Chocolate Buttercream

Yield: 3 cups (645 g) **Prep time:** 15 minutes

A friend once described this buttercream as "the kind you have to put in the sink and cover with water to stop yourself from eating the whole entire bowl." I think she's right, because time and time again I find myself stealing spoonfuls of this frosting while simultaneously decorating a cake with it. I'm a huge fan of all things chocolate, so it's not surprising that this is my favorite buttercream of all. It's silky smooth, easy to whip up and has a rich chocolate flavor without being overly sweet. Pair it with my One-Bowl Chocolate Cake (page 125) for the dreamiest chocolate cake ever.

1 cup (226 g) unsalted butter, at room temperature

3 cups (360 g) powdered sugar

½ cup (45 g) natural unsweetened cocoa powder

2 tbsp (30 ml) whole milk, at room temperature

2 tsp (10 ml) pure vanilla extract

¼ tsp salt

1. In the bowl of a stand mixer fitted with the paddle attachment, whip the butter at high speed for about 4 minutes, until it is creamy and light in color.

2. Scrape the bowl and paddle, then add the powdered sugar, cocoa powder, milk, vanilla and salt. Mix the ingredients at low speed for 1 to 2 minutes, scraping the bowl and paddle halfway through the mixing time, until the ingredients are well incorporated.

Vanilla Buttercream

Yield: 3 cups (645 g)   **Prep time:** 20 minutes

It's essential that you find a great vanilla buttercream recipe that you can depend on for filling and crumb coating cakes, frosting them smooth and piping all the finishing touches. This is my go-to recipe, and over the years I've probably made it thousands of times. Not only is it extremely functional as a frosting and easily pipeable, but it also tastes like a dream, which is equally important! It's packed with vanilla flavor, it's not overly sweet and it is naturally whiter in color due to the extensive whipping of the butter in the first step. You can tint this buttercream (page 47), customize the consistency (page 44) and pair it with just about any cake recipe.

1 cup (226 g) unsalted butter, at room temperature

3½ cups (420 g) powdered sugar

2 tsp (10 ml) pure vanilla extract

2 tbsp (30 ml) whole milk, at room temperature

¼ tsp salt, or as needed

1. In the bowl of a stand mixer fitted with the paddle attachment, cream the butter at high speed for about 7 minutes, until it's creamy and almost white in color.

2. Decrease the mixer's speed to low and add the powdered sugar 1 cup (120 g) at a time, scraping down the bowl and paddle after each addition and making sure each addition is fully incorporated before adding the next.

3. Add the vanilla, milk and salt and mix the ingredients at low speed for 1 minute, until the ingredients are fully incorporated and the frosting is smooth.

Chocolate Ganache Drip

Yield: ¾ cup (180 ml)   **Prep time:** 10 minutes   **Cooling time:** 10–20 minutes

If you've never made chocolate ganache before—let alone dripped a cake with it—the process can come across as a little intimidating. Even the word ganache *sounds fancy and complicated! Truth be told, there are only two ingredients involved here: chocolate and cream. The biggest challenge with this recipe is getting the ratio of these ingredients just right—too much cream and your ganache will be too runny; too little and it will be thick and gloppy. To get that chocolate-to-cream ratio absolutely perfect, I highly recommend using a kitchen scale to most accurately measure the chocolate. Once you have the recipe down, you can practice nailing that drip technique with the tutorial on page 100.*

½ cup (93 g) semisweet or milk chocolate chips

½ cup (120 ml) heavy cream

1. Place the chocolate chips in a small glass or metal bowl.

2. In a small saucepan over medium-high heat, warm the cream until it just starts to simmer. Look for small bubbles forming around the edges and a gentle simmering movement in the middle. When it has reached this point, pour the cream into the bowl of chocolate chips.

3. Whisk the chocolate chips and cream together until the mixture is uniform in consistency and there are no bits of chocolate left on the whisk. Allow the ganache to cool at room temperature for 10 to 20 minutes, or until the ganache is room temperature or slightly above, before using it as a drip.

NOTES

This recipe is written for semisweet chocolate or milk chocolate, both of which require a 1:1 ratio; that is, one part chocolate to one part heavy cream. Since other kinds of chocolate contain different amounts of cocoa solids, they will require a different ratio for best results.

White chocolate: My favorite ratio is 3:1, meaning three parts white chocolate to one part heavy whipping cream. See page 136 for my White Chocolate Ganache Drip.

Dark chocolate: Use a 1:1 ratio, but add an extra 2 tablespoons (30 ml) of heavy cream. Since dark chocolate contains more cocoa solids, it tends to set harder and is prone to cracking if it's not balanced with more cream.

White Chocolate Ganache Drip

Yield: ¾ cup (180 ml)   **Prep time:** 10 minutes   **Cooling time:** 10–20 minutes

White chocolate ganache is the most versatile of all ganaches when it comes to color. Since it's naturally light yellow in color, it's easy to transform it into bold and beautiful hues just by mixing in a few drops of food coloring gel. If you'd rather have a bright white drip, simply add whitening gel to lighten the ganache. Like other types of ganache, it does take some practice and patience to master the consistency and drip technique. Once you get the hang of it, white chocolate ganache will open up a whole new world of creative cake possibilities and color combinations.

1 cup plus 1 tbsp (185 g) white chocolate chips, finely chopped

⅓ cup (80 ml) heavy cream

½ tsp food coloring gel or whitening gel (optional; I use AmeriColor Soft Gel Paste in Bright White)

1. Place the white chocolate chips in a small glass or metal bowl.

2. Pour the cream into a small saucepan over medium-high heat and whisk the cream constantly until it just starts to simmer. Look for small bubbles forming around the edges and a gentle simmering movement in the middle. When the cream has reached this point, turn off the stove and pour the cream over the white chocolate.

3. Whisk the white chocolate and cream together until the ganache is uniform in consistency and there are no bits of white chocolate left on the whisk. If more heat is needed for the white chocolate to melt, carefully hover the bowl over the residual heat from the stove's burner as you whisk.

4. Once the ganache's consistency is uniform, add the food coloring gel or whitening gel (if using) and whisk the ganache until the color is well distributed.

5. Allow the white chocolate ganache to cool at room temperature for 10 to 20 minutes, until it is room temperature or slightly above.

> NOTE
>
> Here are a few keys to success with this recipe: (1) Weigh the white chocolate with a kitchen scale for the most accurate measurement, (2) chop the chocolate finely so it dissolves easily in the cream and (3) be sure to reference "Your Guide to Ganache Drip Cakes" on page 97 to get the technique down.

Salted Caramel

Yield: 1 cup (240 ml)   **Prep time:** 10 minutes   **Cook time:** 10 minutes

This four-ingredient recipe is my go-to caramel for so many reasons: It's quick and easy, highly reliable, tastes incredible and, unlike many salted caramel recipes, it doesn't require a candy thermometer. As long as you follow these detailed instructions and keep a kitchen timer handy, you'll have glorious salted caramel by the end. My biggest tips for success are to read through the recipe first so you know what to expect, have all the ingredients premeasured before you start and make sure you use room-temperature ingredients. When you're finished, you'll be able to use this delicious caramel as a drip, drizzle it between cake layers and even whip it up into Salted Caramel Buttercream (page 206)!

1 cup (200 g) granulated sugar

6 tbsp (84 g) unsalted butter, at room temperature and cubed

½ cup (120 ml) heavy cream, at room temperature

1¼ tsp (8 g) salt (see Note)

1. Make sure all the ingredients are premeasured and within reach, as you'll be constantly stirring. Place the sugar in a medium saucepan over medium-high heat and stir it constantly with a wooden spoon for 5 to 6 minutes, until it melts into an amber-colored liquid and no sugar clumps remain. Be careful to move quickly once the last clump of sugar dissolves, so that the liquid does not burn.

2. Reduce the heat to medium. Carefully add the butter all at once—it will bubble up when you do—and use a whisk to combine it with the sugar liquid for about 2 minutes, until the butter is fully melted and incorporated.

3. Add the cream in a steady stream while whisking constantly. As soon as the cream is incorporated, let the caramel boil for 1 minute without stirring it.

4. Remove the caramel from the heat and stir in the salt.

NOTE

I love kosher salt for this recipe, but you can use any kind of salt that you prefer.

Marshmallow Meringue

Yield: 2 cups (160 g)   **Prep time:** 10 minutes   **Cook time:** 3–4 minutes

This recipe came into my life when I was decorating a s'mores cake for the first time (see Note). I had purchased a jar of marshmallow crème and filled a piping bag with it, expecting to pipe some rosettes on the outside of the cake and toast them. When I realized that the store-bought stuff couldn't hold its shape and instead melted into puddles of goo, I whipped up this recipe to try instead. The results? It pipes beautifully, holds its shape even when toasted, tastes amazing and is versatile. You can use it as cake filling, cover a cake with it, pipe decorations with it, torch it if you want to and spread the extra on some graham crackers to snack on. The only thing to note with this recipe is that you can't make it ahead of time. For the best consistency, make it right before you plan on using it.

2 large egg whites

½ cup (100 g) granulated sugar

¼ tsp cream of tartar

½ tsp pure vanilla extract

1. Fill a medium saucepan with 1 to 2 inches (2.5 to 5 cm) of water and bring it to a simmer over medium heat. Whisk together the egg whites, sugar and cream of tartar in a heatproof bowl, then place the bowl on top of the simmering saucepan. Make sure that the bottom of the bowl does not touch the water. Alternatively, you can use a double boiler for this step.

2. Whisk the egg white mixture constantly for 3 to 4 minutes, until the sugar and cream of tartar are dissolved. The mixture will thin out and be very frothy on top.

3. Remove the mixture from the heat and transfer it to the bowl of a stand mixer fitted with the whisk attachment. Add the vanilla to the egg white mixture, then beat the mixture at high speed for about 5 minutes. It's ready when it looks glossy with stiff peaks. To test it, dip your whisk attachment into the meringue and make sure the peak holds when you lift the whisk out of the meringue.

4. Use the Marshmallow Meringue immediately on cakes, cupcakes or any dessert.

NOTE

You'll find a similar s'mores cake recipe on page 171! The original recipe is at sugarandsparrow.com/smores-cake-recipe.

Chapter 5

NEXT-LEVEL RECIPES

Whether you realized it or not, everything that came before this chapter was preparing you to make these recipes. You've learned how to bake the perfect cake layers, build a structurally sound cake and decorate it in all sorts of ways. You've nailed my essential recipes in the previous chapter and have hopefully already jumped for joy at some cake successes. You're now more than ready for these next-level recipes, and I could not be more excited for you!

These recipes are ones you can reach for whether you want to make someone else's day special or have a great time in the kitchen practicing your skills and making something beautiful with your hands. You'll find flavors here that range from classic to wildly creative, with each cake designed to be challenging yet completely doable: from a celebratory Sprinkle Ombré Funfetti Cake (page 145), to my favorite childhood birthday cake (page 147), to a rainbow-striped creation infused with Lucky Charms™ (page 174), to my Snickerdoodle Cake that's literally rolled in cinnamon sugar (page 166), just to name a few. Every cake in this section comes complete with a full decorating tutorial, so you can make it look just like the picture. But you're always free and encouraged to do your own thing with the final design—feel it out and have fun!

Sprinkle Ombré Funfetti Cake

Yield: 1 triple-layer 6-inch (15-cm) cake or 1 double-layer 8-inch (20-cm) cake
Prep time: 45 minutes   **Bake time:** 32–36 minutes

The most celebratory cake of all, this funfetti cake is an extra light and fluffy vanilla cake with sprinkles baked inside and a delicious Vanilla-Almond Buttercream topping. The buttercream ombré and sprinkle ombré design pictured here is one of my go-tos for parties of all kinds—it is simple to create, yet it's dynamic and eye-catching. To get the look, follow the tutorial for creating an ombré finish (page 78), then add the sprinkles using the techniques on page 106. This cake is perfect in any color palette and is a true crowd-pleaser!

FUNFETTI CAKE

2¾ cups (292 g) sifted cake flour

2 tsp (10 g) baking powder

½ tsp baking soda

1 tsp salt

¾ cup (170 g) unsalted butter, at room temperature

1½ cups (300 g) granulated sugar

2 large eggs plus 2 large egg whites, at room temperature

1 tsp pure almond extract

2 tsp (10 ml) pure vanilla extract

½ cup (120 g) sour cream, at room temperature

1 cup (240 ml) whole milk, at room temperature

½ cup (100 g) rainbow sprinkles, coated in 2 tsp (4 g) cake flour (see Note)

NOTE

The best kind of sprinkles to use inside the cake are rod-shaped ones that don't bleed color. Look for the term confectioner's glaze in the ingredients. I used Sprinkle Pop Ultimate Rainbow sprinkles for these funfetti cake layers.

MAKE THE FUNFETTI CAKE

1. Preheat the oven to 350°F (177°C). Prepare three 6-inch (15-cm) or two 8-inch (20-cm) round cake pans by spraying the sides with baking spray and fitting a parchment paper circle to the bottom of each pan.

2. Place the flour, baking powder, baking soda and salt in a medium bowl and whisk the ingredients to combine them. Set the flour mixture aside.

3. In the bowl of a stand mixer fitted with the paddle attachment, beat the butter at high speed for about 2 minutes, until it is creamy. Add the sugar and mix the ingredients at medium-high speed for 2 minutes, scraping the bowl and paddle at the halfway point. Decrease the mixer's speed to low and add the eggs and egg whites, one at a time, mixing until they are just combined. Add the almond extract, vanilla and sour cream, increase the mixer's speed to high and beat the ingredients for 1 minute.

4. Turn the mixer off and add the flour mixture all at once. Start the mixer at low speed. Mix until the ingredients are just combined, and then, with the mixer still running, slowly pour in the milk. Mix the ingredients at low speed for about 30 seconds, until they are just combined. Scrape the sides and bottom of the bowl and stir the batter with a whisk a few times to make sure there are no lumps. The batter will be slightly thick.

5. Using a rubber spatula, gently fold in the flour-coated sprinkles.

6. Divide the batter evenly between the prepared cake pans. Bake the cakes for 32 to 36 minutes. They're done when they spring back to the touch and a toothpick inserted into the centers comes out clean or with just a few moist crumbs on it. Let the cakes cool in their pans for 5 minutes, then remove them from the pans and allow them to cool completely on a wire rack.

(continued)

Sprinkle Ombré Funfetti Cake *(continued)*

VANILLA-ALMOND BUTTERCREAM

2 cups (452 g) unsalted butter, at room temperature

7 cups (840 g) powdered sugar

1 tbsp (15 ml) pure vanilla extract

1 tsp pure almond extract

4 tbsp (60 ml) whole milk, at room temperature

¼ tsp salt, or as needed

AmeriColor Soft Gel Paste in Deep Pink

TOPPING

½ cup (100 g) Sprinkle Pop Rainbow Road sprinkles, divided

MAKE THE VANILLA-ALMOND BUTTERCREAM

1. In the bowl of a stand mixer fitted with the paddle attachment, beat the butter at medium-high speed for about 7 minutes, until it's creamy and almost white in color.

2. Decrease the mixer's speed to low and add the powdered sugar 2 cups (240 g) at a time, scraping the bowl and paddle after each addition.

3. Add the vanilla, almond extract, milk and salt and mix the ingredients at low speed for 1 to 2 minutes, until the ingredients are fully incorporated and the frosting is smooth.

4. If you'll be tinting the buttercream for an ombré finish, wait until step 2 of the assembly instructions to add the food coloring gel.

ASSEMBLE THE CAKE

1. Level the cooled cake layers to your desired height (page 31). Fill and stack the cake layers (page 32) with Vanilla-Almond Buttercream, then crumb coat the cake (page 37) with Vanilla-Almond Buttercream. Chill the crumb-coated cake in the refrigerator for at least 30 minutes to allow the frosting to firm up.

2. Mix the buttercream ombré color palette. Divide the remaining Vanilla-Almond Buttercream between three bowls: Use 2½ cups (538 g) of buttercream for the darkest color, ¾ cup (161 g) of buttercream for the in-between color and 1½ cups (323 g) of buttercream for the lightest color. Mix 4 to 5 drops of AmeriColor Deep Pink into the bowl with 2½ cups (538 g) of buttercream to create the darkest color. Next, add about 2 tablespoons (26 g) of the darkest buttercream to the bowl with ¾ cup (161 g) of buttercream to create the in-between color. Leave the third bowl of buttercream uncolored.

3. Use the buttercream from the previous step to create an ombré finish (page 77), then use about ⅓ cup (67 g) of the sprinkles to add a sprinkle border (page 106) and floating sprinkles (page 107) to the sides of the cake.

4. Mix all of the remaining buttercream together and use it to create a swirl border (page 116) around the top of the cake with a Wilton tip 4B. Garnish the swirls with the remaining sprinkles.

Classic Birthday Cake

Yield: 1 triple-layer 6-inch (15-cm) cake or 1 double-layer 8-inch (20-cm) cake
Prep time: 40 minutes   **Cook time:** 30–35 minutes

For the majority of my childhood birthdays, my mom would bake a store-bought yellow cake mix in a casserole dish, frost it with canned chocolate frosting and add rainbow sprinkles on top. Yellow cake is the height of nostalgia for me, always bringing me right back to the backyard birthday parties of my grade school years. To replicate the boxed cake mix texture I love so much, this recipe uses vegetable oil and sour cream for added moisture, which is balanced with cake flour to make the crumb oh-so-light. Its natural yellow coloring comes from the egg yolks in the recipe (see Tip). Pair this classic cake with decadent Chocolate Buttercream (page 132) and rainbow sprinkles to make anyone's birthday special!

YELLOW CAKE

2½ cups (265 g) sifted cake flour

2 tsp (10 g) baking powder

½ tsp baking soda

½ tsp salt

¾ cup (170 g) unsalted butter, at room temperature

¼ cup (60 ml) vegetable oil

1⅔ cups (332 g) granulated sugar

3 large eggs plus 1 large egg yolk, at room temperature

⅓ cup (80 g) sour cream, at room temperature

1 tbsp (15 ml) pure vanilla extract

1 cup (240 ml) whole milk, at room temperature

MAKE THE YELLOW CAKE

1. Preheat the oven to 350°F (177°C). Prepare three 6-inch (15-cm) or two 8-inch (20-cm) round cake pans by spraying the sides with baking spray and fitting a parchment paper circle to the bottom of each pan.

2. In a medium bowl, whisk together the flour, baking powder, baking soda and salt. Set the flour mixture aside.

3. In the bowl of a stand mixer fitted with the paddle attachment, beat the butter at high speed for 2 minutes, until it is light and creamy. Add the oil and sugar, then mix the ingredients at medium-high speed for 2 minutes, scraping the bowl and paddle at the halfway point. Decrease the mixer's speed to low and add the eggs and egg yolk, one at a time, mixing until the ingredients are just combined and scraping the bowl and paddle as needed. Add the sour cream and vanilla, increase the mixer's speed to high and beat the ingredients for 1 minute. The mixture will look curdled at this point, but don't worry—it will become smooth at the end.

4. Turn the mixer off and add the flour mixture all at once. Start the mixer at low speed. Mix the ingredients until they are just combined, then add the milk in a steady stream. Mix until the milk is just incorporated. Scrape the sides and bottom of the bowl and stir the batter a few times to make sure there are no lumps. The batter will be slightly thick.

5. Divide the batter evenly between the prepared cake pans. Bake the cakes for 30 to 35 minutes. They're done when they spring back to the touch and a toothpick inserted into the centers comes out clean. Let the cakes cool in their pans for 5 minutes, then remove them from the pans and allow them to cool completely on a wire rack.

(continued)

CHOCOLATE BUTTERCREAM

2 batches Chocolate Buttercream
(page 132)

TOPPING

½ cup (100 g) rainbow sprinkles

MAKE THE CHOCOLATE BUTTERCREAM

1. Make 2 batches of the Chocolate Buttercream (page 132).

ASSEMBLE THE CAKE

1. Level the cooled cake layers to your desired height (page 31). Fill and stack the layers (page 32) with Chocolate Buttercream, then crumb coat the cake (page 37) with Chocolate Buttercream. Chill the crumb-coated cake in the refrigerator for at least 30 minutes to allow the frosting to firm up.

2. Frost a smooth buttercream finish (page 61) with Chocolate Buttercream, then add a sprinkle border (page 106) and floating sprinkles (page 107) to the sides of the cake using the rainbow sprinkles.

3. With the remaining Chocolate Buttercream, pipe a swirl border (page 116) with a Wilton tip 4B, then garnish the swirls with more rainbow sprinkles.

TIP:

If you want the most vibrant yellow cake, look for the term "pasture-raised" on your eggs' label—the color of those yolks tends to be the most saturated of all!

Double Chocolate & Peanut Butter Cake

Yield: 1 triple-layer 6-inch (15-cm) cake or 1 double-layer 8-inch (20-cm) cake
Prep time: 35 minutes   **Bake time:** 32–36 minutes

If you're looking for comfort in a cake, you have come to the right page. This cake is as indulgent as the name implies: layers of extra fudgy chocolate cake with peanut butter–infused chocolate buttercream. It's the kind of cake you can throw together for a cozy weekend of binge-watching your favorite show. Or you can just as easily dress it up with some rustic swirls (page 85) and brighten someone's day. It's quick, easy and always a good idea!

FUDGY CHOCOLATE CAKE

2 cups (266 g) all-purpose flour

1⅔ cups (332 g) granulated sugar

⅔ cup (60 g) natural unsweetened cocoa powder

2 tsp (10 g) baking soda

1 tsp baking powder

½ tsp salt

½ cup (120 ml) vegetable oil

2 large eggs, at room temperature

¾ cup (180 g) sour cream, at room temperature

1½ tsp (8 ml) pure vanilla extract

½ cup (120 ml) full-fat buttermilk, at room temperature

½ cup (120 ml) hot coffee (see Note)

CHOCOLATE-PEANUT BUTTER FROSTING

1½ cups (339 g) unsalted butter, at room temperature

⅓ cup (83 g) creamy peanut butter

4½ cups (540 g) powdered sugar

¾ cup (68 g) natural unsweetened cocoa powder

6 tbsp (90 ml) whole milk, at room temperature

1 tbsp (15 ml) pure vanilla extract

½ tsp salt

MAKE THE FUDGY CHOCOLATE CAKE

1. Preheat the oven to 350°F (177°C). Prepare three 6-inch (15-cm) or two 8-inch (20-cm) round cake pans by spraying the sides with baking spray and fitting a parchment paper circle to the bottom of each pan.

2. In the bowl of a stand mixer fitted with the paddle attachment, combine the flour, granulated sugar, cocoa powder, baking soda, baking powder and salt. Stir the ingredients together at low speed for 30 seconds to fully combine them. Add the oil, eggs, sour cream, vanilla and buttermilk and mix the ingredients at low speed until they are just combined. With the mixer still running at low speed, add the coffee in a slow stream. After adding the coffee, mix the batter for 1 to 2 minutes, until the ingredients are fully combined. The batter will be very thin.

3. Divide the batter evenly between the prepared cake pans. Bake the cakes for 32 to 36 minutes, until a toothpick inserted into the centers comes out clean. Let the cakes cool in their pans for 5 minutes, then remove them from the pans and allow them to cool completely on a wire rack.

MAKE THE CHOCOLATE-PEANUT BUTTER FROSTING

1. In the bowl of a stand mixer fitted with the paddle attachment, whip the butter and peanut butter together at medium speed for about 3 minutes, until the mixture is very creamy and the two are well combined.

2. Decrease the mixer's speed to low and add the powdered sugar, cocoa powder, milk, vanilla and salt and mix the ingredients together for 2 to 3 minutes, scraping the bowl and paddle as needed, until the ingredients are fully combined.

(continued)

Double Chocolate & Peanut Butter Cake *(continued)*

8 Reese's Miniature peanut butter cups

ASSEMBLE THE CAKE

1. Level the cooled cake layers to your desired height (page 31). Fill and stack the layers (page 32) with Chocolate–Peanut Butter Frosting, then crumb coat the cake (page 37) with Chocolate–Peanut Butter Frosting. Chill the crumb-coated cake in the refrigerator for at least 30 minutes to allow the frosting to firm up.

2. Create a rustic swirl finish (page 85) with the remaining Chocolate–Peanut Butter Frosting.

3. Cut 2 of the Reese's Miniature peanut butter cups into quarters. Cut 2 peanut butter cups in half. Place the quartered and halved peanut butter cups, along with the 4 whole peanut butter cups, on top of the cake as a garnish.

NOTE

The addition of hot coffee will deepen the chocolate flavor in this cake; thus, I highly recommend it. If you'd rather not use coffee, you may use an equal amount of hot water instead.

Chocolate Mocha Cake

Yield: 1 triple-layer 6-inch (15-cm) cake or 1 double-layer 8-inch (20-cm) cake
Prep time: 45 minutes   **Bake time:** 32–36 minutes

I've always considered a mocha to be more of a midday treat than a morning ritual, so I was sure the flavors would come together quite nicely in cake form. Turns out that this cake is more than nice—the flavor combination is complex, sophisticated and insanely delicious! Coffee naturally amplifies the chocolate flavor, and when you add that to the moist and fudgy crumb and the delightful Mocha Buttercream, you're in for a rich and satisfying experience that might even put a little pep in your step.

CHOCOLATE MOCHA CAKE

2 cups (266 g) all-purpose flour

1⅔ cups (332 g) granulated sugar

⅔ cup (60 g) natural unsweetened cocoa powder

2 tsp (10 g) baking soda

1 tsp baking powder

2 tsp (2 g) espresso powder

½ tsp salt

½ cup (120 ml) vegetable oil

2 large eggs, at room temperature

1½ tsp (8 ml) pure vanilla extract

1 cup (240 ml) full-fat buttermilk, at room temperature

1 cup (240 ml) hot coffee

MAKE THE CHOCOLATE MOCHA CAKE

1. Preheat the oven to 350°F (177°C). Prepare three 6-inch (15-cm) or two 8-inch (20-cm) round cake pans by spraying the sides with baking spray and fitting a parchment paper circle to the bottom of each pan.

2. In the bowl of a stand mixer fitted with the paddle attachment, combine the flour, granulated sugar, cocoa powder, baking soda, baking powder, espresso powder and salt. Stir the ingredients together at low speed for 30 seconds to fully combine them. Add the oil, eggs, vanilla and buttermilk and mix the ingredients at low speed until they are just combined. With the mixer still at low speed, add the coffee in a slow stream. After adding the coffee, mix the ingredients at low speed for 1 to 2 minutes, until they are fully combined. The batter will be very thin.

3. Divide the batter between the prepared cake pans. Bake the cakes for 32 to 36 minutes, until a toothpick inserted into the centers comes out clean. Let the cakes cool in their pans for 5 minutes, then remove them from the pans and allow them to cool completely on a wire rack.

(continued)

Chocolate Mocha Cake *(continued)*

MOCHA BUTTERCREAM

2 cups (452 g) unsalted butter, at room temperature

7 cups (840 g) powdered sugar

⅓ cup (30g) natural unsweetened cocoa powder

1 tbsp (3 g) instant coffee or espresso powder

4 tbsp (60 ml) whole milk, at room temperature

2 tsp (10 ml) pure vanilla extract

¼ tsp salt, or as needed

TOPPING

Chocolate-covered espresso beans, as needed

MAKE THE MOCHA BUTTERCREAM

1. In the bowl of a stand mixer fitted with the paddle attachment, cream the butter at medium-high speed for about 5 minutes, scraping the bowl and paddle frequently, until it is light and fluffy. Turn off the mixer.

2. In a large bowl, whisk together the powdered sugar and cocoa powder. Turn the mixer to low speed and add the powdered sugar mixture to the creamed butter 2 cups (240 g) at a time, scraping the bowl and paddle between each addition. Turn off the stand mixer.

3. In a small bowl, combine the instant coffee and milk. Add the coffee-milk mixture to the butter-sugar mixture, then add the vanilla and salt. Mix the ingredients at low speed for 1 to 2 minutes, scraping the bowl and paddle as needed, until the ingredients are fully incorporated and the frosting is smooth.

ASSEMBLE THE CAKE

1. Level the cooled cake layers to your desired height (page 31). Fill and stack the layers (page 32) with Mocha Buttercream, then crumb coat the cake (page 37) with Mocha Buttercream. Chill the crumb-coated cake in the refrigerator for at least 30 minutes to allow the frosting to firm up.

2. Reserve 1½ cups (323 g) of the Mocha Buttercream for the swirl border, then create a textured finish of symmetrical textures or rustic swirls (pages 84–85) with the remaining Mocha Buttercream.

3. Use the reserved Mocha Buttercream to pipe a swirl border (page 116) around the top of the cake with a Wilton tip 2D. Top each swirl with the chocolate-covered espresso beans.

White Chocolate Chai Cake with White Chocolate Drip

Yield: 1 triple-layer 6-inch (15-cm) cake or 1 double-layer 8-inch (20-cm) cake
Prep time: 1 hour 5 minutes   **Bake time:** 30–35 minutes

This heavenly recipe combines two of my all-time most popular blog recipes—Spiced Vanilla Chai Cake and White Chocolate Buttercream—into one tasty cake! For this recipe, I pair layers of chai tea–infused cake with spiced white chocolate buttercream for the dreamiest tea-inspired cake. Top the cake with White Chocolate Ganache Drip, crumbled Lotus Biscoff Cookies and a braided buttercream border (page 116), and it becomes an elegant centerpiece for your next gathering. The one challenge with this recipe is ensuring that the White Chocolate Ganache Drip is bright white while maintaining the perfect consistency for the drip. Be sure to reference page 97 for helpful tips. Also, if you'd rather have a more traditional chai cake, add 1 tablespoon (15 g) of my Chai Spice Mix to a double batch of my Vanilla Buttercream (page 133) and use it as a substitute for the White Chocolate Chai Buttercream in this recipe. All fans of chai tea will adore this cake!

CHAI SPICE MIX

4 tsp (10 g) ground cinnamon

2 tsp (3 g) ground ginger

1 tsp ground cardamom

½ tsp ground allspice

¼ tsp ground cloves

CHAI CAKE

1 (0.11-oz [3-g]) chai tea bag

1 cup (240 ml) whole milk

2¾ cups (292 g) sifted cake flour

2 tsp (10 g) baking powder

½ tsp baking soda

4 tsp (20 g) Chai Spice Mix

1 tsp salt

¾ cup (170 g) unsalted butter, at room temperature

1½ cups (300 g) granulated sugar

3 large eggs, at room temperature

½ cup (120 g) sour cream, at room temperature

1 tbsp (15 ml) pure vanilla extract

MAKE THE CHAI SPICE MIX

1. In a small bowl, whisk together the cinnamon, ginger, cardamom, allspice and cloves. Set the Chai Spice Mix aside.

MAKE THE CHAI CAKE

1. Preheat the oven to 350°F (177°C). Prepare three 6-inch (15-cm) or two 8-inch (20-cm) round cake pans by spraying the sides with baking spray and fitting a parchment paper circle to the bottom of each pan.

2. Place the chai tea bag in a medium Mason jar. In a small saucepan over medium-high heat, warm the milk, stirring it constantly, until it begins to boil. Pour the boiling milk into the Mason jar and let the tea bag steep for 20 minutes, then remove it. Allow the tea-infused milk to cool completely before moving on to step 3.

3. In a medium bowl, combine the flour, baking powder, baking soda, Chai Spice Mix and salt. Whisk the ingredients to combine them. Set the flour mixture aside.

4. In the bowl of your stand mixer fitted with the paddle attachment, beat the butter at high speed for 2 minutes, until it is light and fluffy. Add the granulated sugar and mix the ingredients at medium-high speed for 2 minutes, scraping the bowl and paddle as needed. Add the eggs one at a time. Add the sour cream and vanilla and mix the ingredients at high speed for 1 minute, scraping the bowl and paddle once during the mixing time.

(continued)

WHITE CHOCOLATE CHAI BUTTERCREAM

2 cups (340g) white chocolate chips

2 cups (452 g) unsalted butter, at room temperature

3 cups (360 g) powdered sugar

1 tbsp (15 g) Chai Spice Mix

2 tsp (10 ml) pure vanilla extract

¼ tsp salt

5. With the mixer running at low speed, add the flour mixture and mix the ingredients until they are just combined. Add the chai milk mixture slowly and mix the ingredients until the milk is just incorporated. Scrape the sides and bottom of the bowl and stir the batter a few times to make sure there are no lumps. The batter will be slightly thick.

6. Divide the batter evenly between the prepared cake pans. Bake the cakes for 30 to 35 minutes. They're done when they spring back to the touch and a toothpick inserted into the centers comes out clean. Let the cakes cool in their pans for 5 minutes, then remove them from the pans and allow them to cool completely on a wire rack.

MAKE THE WHITE CHOCOLATE CHAI BUTTERCREAM

1. Place the white chocolate chips in a glass bowl and microwave them in 20-second intervals, stirring the chocolate chips after each interval, until they are melted and smooth. It should take three or four intervals to reach this stage. Alternatively, you can melt the white chocolate in a double boiler. Once the white chocolate is melted, set it aside to cool.

2. In the bowl of a stand mixer fitted with a paddle attachment, beat the butter at high speed for about 4 minutes, until it is light and creamy. Decrease the mixer's speed to low, add the powdered sugar and mix the ingredients until they are well combined. Scrape the bowl and paddle. Stir the melted white chocolate a few times and make sure it's not hot enough to melt the butter—if it is still too hot, let it cool for a few more minutes. Add the white chocolate to the butter mixture. Increase the mixer's speed to medium and beat the ingredients for 2 minutes, until the mixture is smooth.

3. Add the Chai Spice Mix, vanilla and salt. Mix the buttercream at low speed for 1 minute to fully combine the ingredients.

½ cup (186 g) crushed Lotus Biscoff Cookies, divided

1 batch White Chocolate Ganache Drip (page 136)

5 whole star anise

ASSEMBLE THE CAKE

1. Level the cooled cake layers to your desired height (page 31). Fill and stack the cake layers (page 32) with the White Chocolate Chai Buttercream, then crumb coat the cake (page 37) with White Chocolate Chai Buttercream. Chill the crumb-coated cake in the refrigerator for at least 30 minutes to allow the frosting to firm up.

2. Create a smooth buttercream finish (page 61) with White Chocolate Chai Buttercream. Press about ⅓ cup (124 g) of the crushed Lotus Biscoff Cookies around the bottom edge of the cake using the palm of your hand, then refrigerate the cake for 20 minutes while you prepare the White Chocolate Ganache Drip (page 136).

3. When the White Chocolate Ganache Drip has reached the ideal consistency, create a traditional drip (page 100) around the top edge of the cake. Chill the cake in the refrigerator for at least 5 minutes to allow the ganache to set.

4. Using the remaining White Chocolate Chai Buttercream, create a braided border (page 116) with a Wilton tip 4B around the top edge of the cake. Garnish the cake by sprinkling it with the remaining crushed cookies and placing the star anise on top of the braided buttercream.

Striped Strawberry Matcha Cake

Yield: 1 triple-layer 6-inch (15-cm) cake or 1 double-layer 8-inch (20-cm) cake
Prep time: 1 hour   **Bake time:** 30–35 minutes

I love a good matcha latte, but I love baking with matcha even more. It has a unique, earthy flavor profile that can seem bitter on its own, but after balancing it with the sweetness of a cake recipe and the right contrasting flavors, it's absolutely delightful. This cake is the perfect example: layers of soft and fluffy matcha cake contrasted with sweet Strawberry Buttercream and Vanilla Buttercream to round it all out. One key to success with this one: Make sure to use culinary-grade matcha powder in the cake—it's higher quality than ceremonial-grade matcha and gives the finished product a bolder flavor.

MATCHA CAKE

2¾ cups (292 g) sifted cake flour

2 tbsp (12 g) culinary-grade matcha powder

2 tsp (10 g) baking powder

½ tsp baking soda

½ tsp salt

¾ cup (170 g) unsalted butter, at room temperature

1⅔ cups (332 g) granulated sugar

3 large eggs, at room temperature

½ cup (120 g) sour cream, at room temperature

2 tsp (10 ml) pure vanilla extract

1 cup (240 ml) whole milk, at room temperature

MAKE THE MATCHA CAKE

1. Preheat the oven to 350°F (177°C). Prepare three 6-inch (15-cm) or two 8-inch (20-cm) round cake pans by spraying the sides with baking spray and fitting a parchment paper circle to the bottom of each pan.

2. In a medium bowl, whisk together the flour, matcha powder, baking powder, baking soda and salt. Set the flour mixture aside.

3. In the bowl of a stand mixer fitted with the paddle attachment, beat the butter at high speed for 2 minutes, until it is light and creamy. Add the granulated sugar and cream the butter and sugar together at medium-high speed for 2 minutes. Decrease the mixer's speed to low and add the eggs one at a time, mixing until the ingredients are just combined and scraping the bowl and paddle as needed. Add the sour cream and vanilla, increase the mixer's speed to high and beat the mixture for 1 minute. It will look curdled at this point, but don't worry—it will become smooth at the end.

4. Turn the mixer off and add the flour mixture all at once. Start the mixer at low speed. Mix the ingredients until they are just combined, then slowly pour in the milk. Continue to mix the ingredients at low speed for about 30 seconds, until they are just combined. Scrape the sides and bottom of the bowl and stir the batter with a whisk a few times to make sure there are no lumps. The batter will be slightly thick.

5. Divide the batter evenly between the prepared cake pans. Bake the cakes for 30 to 35 minutes. They're done when they spring back to the touch and a toothpick inserted into the centers comes out clean. Let the cakes cool in their pans for 5 minutes, then remove them from the pans and allow them to cool completely on a wire rack.

(continued)

STRAWBERRY BUTTERCREAM

1½ cups (26 g) freeze-dried strawberries (see Note)

1½ cups (339 g) unsalted butter, at room temperature

4 tbsp (60 ml) whole milk, at room temperature

1½ tsp (8 ml) pure vanilla extract

5¼ cups (630 g) powdered sugar

¼ tsp salt

VANILLA BUTTERCREAM

1 batch Vanilla Buttercream (page 133)

1–2 tsp (2–4 g) culinary-grade matcha powder

TOPPINGS

Sliced fresh strawberries, as needed

MAKE THE STRAWBERRY BUTTERCREAM

1. Using a food processor, grind the freeze-dried strawberries into a fine powder—you'll end up with about ⅓ cup (6 g) of strawberry powder. In the bowl of a stand mixer fitted with the paddle attachment, whip the butter at medium speed for about 5 minutes, until it's creamy and light in color. Add the milk, vanilla and strawberry powder and mix for 1 minute.

2. Decrease the mixer's speed to low and add the powdered sugar 2 cups (240 g) at a time, mixing the ingredients well and scraping the bowl after each addition. Add the salt and mix at low speed for 1 minute, until the ingredients are well combined and the frosting is smooth.

MAKE THE VANILLA BUTTERCREAM

1. Make 1 batch of Vanilla Buttercream (page 133). Set the frosting aside.

ASSEMBLE THE CAKE

1. Level the cooled cake layers to your desired height (page 31). Fill and stack the cake layers (page 32) with Strawberry Buttercream. Crumb coat the cake (page 37) with Strawberry Buttercream. Chill the crumb-coated cake in the refrigerator for at least 30 minutes to allow the frosting to set up.

2. Follow the tutorial on page 88 to create a striped finish with the Vanilla Buttercream and Strawberry Buttercream. Begin the striping process with the Vanilla Buttercream. After using the cake comb to create the grooves, fill them with Strawberry Buttercream.

3. Divide the remaining Vanilla Buttercream equally between two bowls. Add the matcha powder to one of the bowls to create a green buttercream. Use the two colors of Vanilla Buttercream and the Strawberry Buttercream to create a crescent border (page 116) of piped rosettes and stars. As an optional addition, you can do the same effect on a lower area on the side of the cake. Finish by adding sliced fresh strawberries within the piped rosettes and stars.

NOTE

Freeze-dried strawberries are not the same as frozen strawberries. The process of freeze-drying removes all of the liquid from the berries and amplifies the flavor, making them perfect for flavoring buttercream without altering the consistency. Look for them next to raisins and other dried fruit at your local grocery store.

Vintage Piped Red Velvet Cake

Yield: 1 triple-layer 6-inch (15-cm) cake or 1 double-layer 8-inch (20-cm) cake
Prep time: 55 minutes   **Bake time:** 30–35 minutes

I've always thought of red velvet as a fancy cake, so dressing it up with this vintage Lambeth-style buttercream piping seemed more than fitting! This famous cake is flavored with just a hint of cocoa powder, made extra moist and fluffy with buttermilk and cake flour and is tinted red using food coloring gel for that classic look. Here are my tips for success for this recipe: First, I recommend using a highly concentrated food coloring gel like AmeriColor Soft Gel Paste in Super Red. This way, you won't have to use a lot of food coloring. Second, to make sure your Lambeth piping looks perfectly detailed, check your buttercream consistency and, if necessary, thicken it slightly before piping—page 44 shows you how!

RED VELVET CAKE

2½ cups (265 g) sifted cake flour

2 tbsp (12 g) natural unsweetened cocoa powder

1 tsp baking soda

½ tsp salt

½ cup (113 g) unsalted butter, at room temperature

1½ cups (300 g) granulated sugar

½ cup (120 ml) vegetable oil

2 large eggs, at room temperature

2 tsp (10 ml) pure vanilla extract

1 tsp distilled white vinegar

1 tbsp (15 ml) AmeriColor Soft Gel Paste in Super Red

1 cup (240 ml) full-fat buttermilk, at room temperature

MAKE THE RED VELVET CAKE

1. Preheat the oven to 350°F (177°C). Prepare three 6-inch (15-cm) or two 8-inch (20-cm) round cake pans by spraying the sides with baking spray and fitting a parchment paper circle to the bottom of each pan.

2. In a medium bowl, whisk together the flour, cocoa powder, baking soda and salt. Set the flour mixture aside.

3. In the bowl of a stand mixer fitted with the paddle attachment, cream the butter at high speed for 2 minutes, then add the sugar and oil. Cream the ingredients together at medium-high speed for about 2 minutes, until the mixture is light and fluffy. Scrape the bowl and paddle. Turn the mixer to low speed and add the eggs one at a time. When the eggs are incorporated, add the vanilla and vinegar and mix the ingredients at low speed for 30 seconds. Scrape the bowl and paddle once more.

4. In a small bowl, mix the red food coloring gel into the buttermilk. With the mixer running at low speed, alternate adding the flour mixture and buttermilk in three additions, beginning and ending with the flour mixture. Mix only until the ingredients start to come together, then whisk the batter by hand a few times to make sure there are no large lumps.

5. Divide the batter between the prepared cake pans. Bake the cakes for 30 to 35 minutes, until a toothpick inserted into the centers comes out clean. Let the cakes cool in their pans for 5 minutes, then remove them from the pans and allow them to cool completely on a wire rack.

(continued)

Vintage Piped Red Velvet Cake *(continued)*

CREAM CHEESE BUTTERCREAM

3 batches Cream Cheese Buttercream (page 130; see Note)

AmeriColor Soft Gel Paste in Dusty Rose (optional)

MAKE THE CREAM CHEESE BUTTERCREAM

1. Make a triple batch of the Cream Cheese Buttercream (page 130). If desired, tint the Cream Cheese Buttercream with 4 or 5 drops of AmeriColor Dusty Rose.

ASSEMBLE THE CAKE

1. Level the cooled cake layers to your desired height (page 31). Fill and stack the cake layers (page 32) with the Cream Cheese Buttercream, then crumb coat the cake (page 37) with Cream Cheese Buttercream. Chill the crumb-coated cake in the refrigerator for at least 30 minutes to allow the frosting to firm up.

2. Frost a smooth buttercream finish (page 61) with Cream Cheese Buttercream, then refrigerate the cake for 20 minutes to allow the frosting to firm up.

3. Use the remaining Cream Cheese Buttercream to decorate the cake with Lambeth piping (page 91).

> NOTE
>
> A triple batch of Cream Cheese Buttercream yields enough for filling, frosting and piping the Lambeth textures. If you're not planning on replicating the Lambeth design in the tutorial on page 92, a double batch of Cream Cheese Buttercream will yield enough to fill, frost and decorate the cake with a simple buttercream border.

Snickerdoodle Cake

Yield: 1 triple-layer 6-inch (15-cm) cake or 1 double-layer 8-inch (20-cm) cake
Prep time: 55 minutes   **Bake time:** 35–40 minutes

This recipe captures all the best aspects of a snickerdoodle cookie to make the ultimate cake version! It starts with an extra-soft, cinnamon-sugar marbled vanilla cake that will make your kitchen smell like heaven. You'll fill and frost those beautiful cake layers with Cinnamon–Brown Sugar Buttercream, then you'll roll the entire cake in cinnamon sugar to coat it just like a snickerdoodle! Finish the look with a star border (page 116) to make the cake extra cute. If you're a fan of snickerdoodle cookies, you'll be over the moon for this cake.

SNICKERDOODLE CAKE

2½ cups (265g) sifted cake flour

2 tsp (10 g) baking powder

½ tsp salt

¾ cup (170 g) unsalted butter, at room temperature

¼ cup (60 ml) vegetable oil

1½ cups (300 g) granulated sugar

3 large eggs, at room temperature

¼ cup (60 g) sour cream, at room temperature

1 tbsp (15 ml) pure vanilla extract

1 cup (240 ml) whole milk, at room temperature

CINNAMON-SUGAR RIBBON

⅓ cup (67 g) packed light or dark brown sugar

¼ cup (30 g) unsifted cake flour

2 tsp (5 g) ground cinnamon

3 tbsp (42 g) unsalted butter, melted

MAKE THE SNICKERDOODLE CAKE

1. Preheat the oven to 350°F (177°C). Prepare three 6-inch (15-cm) or two 8-inch (20-cm) round cake pans by spraying the sides with baking spray and fitting a parchment paper circle to the bottom of each pan.

2. In a medium bowl, whisk the flour, baking powder and salt; set aside.

3. In the bowl of a stand mixer fitted with the paddle attachment, cream together the butter, oil and granulated sugar at medium-high speed for 3 minutes. Scrape the bowl and paddle. With the mixer running at low speed, add the eggs one at a time, scraping the bowl and paddle as needed. Mix just until the last egg is combined. Add the sour cream and vanilla, then beat the mixture at medium speed for 1 minute.

4. Scrape the bowl and paddle. Decrease the mixer's speed to low. Add the flour mixture in three additions, alternating with the milk in two additions. Mix the ingredients until they are just blended. Stir the batter by hand a few times to make sure no large lumps remain.

5. Divide the batter evenly between the prepared cake pans; set aside.

MAKE THE CINNAMON-SUGAR RIBBON

6. In a small bowl, mix together the brown sugar, flour and cinnamon until they are combined. Pour the melted butter on top of the cinnamon-sugar mixture and stir the ingredients until they are just combined.

7. Add spoonfuls of the Cinnamon-Sugar Ribbon to the unbaked cakes and gently swirl it in with a butter knife. Bake the cakes for 35 to 40 minutes. They're done when they spring back to the touch and a toothpick inserted into the centers comes out clean or with a few crumbs. Let the cakes cool in their pans for 5 minutes, then remove them from the pans and cool them on a wire rack.

(continued)

1½ cups (339 g) unsalted butter, at room temperature

¾ cup (150 g) packed brown sugar

5¼ cups (630 g) powdered sugar

1½ tsp (4 g) ground cinnamon

1 tbsp (15 ml) pure vanilla extract

4 tbsp (60 ml) whole milk, at room temperature

¼ tsp salt, or as needed

CINNAMON-SUGAR TOPPING

½ cup (100 g) granulated sugar

1 tbsp (8 g) ground cinnamon

NOTE

It might sound nerve-racking to roll the cake through the Cinnamon-Sugar Topping, but I promise it's not as scary as it sounds. As long as the buttercream is chilled and firm to the touch, it should be an easy and fun process. If you're uncomfortable rolling the cake, you can instead press handfuls of the Cinnamon-Sugar Topping onto the chilled cake with the palm of your hand until it's well covered—just be sure to place a baking sheet underneath the turntable to minimize the mess.

MAKE THE CINNAMON–BROWN SUGAR BUTTERCREAM

1. In the bowl of a stand mixer fitted with the paddle attachment, cream together the butter and brown sugar at medium-high speed for about 4 minutes, until the mixture is creamy and light.

2. Decrease the mixer's speed to low, and then add the powdered sugar 2 cups (240 g) at a time, scraping the bowl and paddle after each addition.

3. Add the cinnamon, vanilla, milk and salt and mix the ingredients together at low speed for 1 minute, until the ingredients are fully incorporated and the frosting is smooth.

ASSEMBLE THE CAKE

1. Level the cooled cake layers to your desired height (page 31). Fill and stack the cake layers (page 32) with Cinnamon–Brown Sugar Buttercream, then crumb coat the cake (page 37) with Cinnamon–Brown Sugar Buttercream. Refrigerate the cake for at least 30 minutes to allow the frosting to firm up.

2. Reserve about 1 cup (215 g) of the Cinnamon–Brown Sugar Buttercream for step 7, then create a smooth buttercream finish (page 61) with the remaining buttercream.

3. Refrigerate the cake for 20 minutes to let the buttercream set up. Meanwhile, make the Cinnamon-Sugar Topping: Place the granulated sugar and cinnamon on a rimmed medium baking sheet. Shake the baking sheet to slightly spread out the sugar and cinnamon and create an even layer for rolling (see Note).

4. When the cake has finished chilling, place a cardboard cake circle the same diameter as the cake on top of it. Run a warm paring knife around the bottom edge of the cake to separate it from the turntable, then use an angled spatula to gently lift the bottom of the cake up. Slip one hand underneath the cake. Place your other hand on the cardboard cake circle you placed on top of the cake and lift the whole thing up (A).

5. Turn the cake so that it is horizontal instead of vertical and gently roll the cake over the baking sheet to cover it in the Cinnamon-Sugar Topping, holding it with both hands the entire time (B). Keep rolling the cake, shaking the baking sheet to disperse the cinnamon sugar between rolls, until the sides are covered (C).

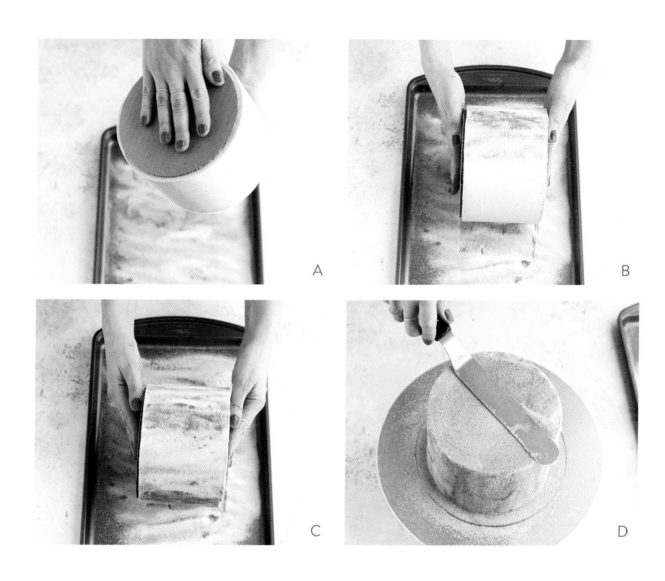

A

B

C

D

6. Place the cake on a turntable and remove the cardboard cake circle you placed on top in step 4. Add 3 to 4 tablespoons (39 to 52 g) of the Cinnamon-Sugar Topping to the top of the cake and smooth it into the buttercream with an angled spatula until the top is fully covered (D).

7. Use the reserved Cinnamon–Brown Sugar Buttercream to pipe a star border (page 116) around the top edge with a Wilton tip 6B.

Toasted Marshmallow S'mores Cake

Yield: 1 triple-layer 6-inch (15-cm) cake or 1 double-layer 8-inch (20-cm) cake
Prep time: 1 hour 20 minutes   **Bake time:** 30–35 minutes

There are so many fun ways to translate the flavors of s'mores into cake form. This is one variation of my s'mores cake that I love (see Notes). It's perfect for the s'mores lover in your life: layers of graham cracker–infused cake and marshmallow-rich buttercream with toasted marshmallow bits folded in, topped with my rich Chocolate Buttercream (page 132) and torched Marshmallow Meringue (page 140). Aside from the fact that this cake is an absolute joy to eat, my favorite part about this recipe is breaking out my kitchen torch to toast that pretty piped Marshmallow Meringue. It's empowering!

GRAHAM CRACKER CAKE

1 cup (104 g) graham cracker crumbs (about 7 whole graham crackers, or 14 squares)

2½ cups (265 g) sifted cake flour

2 tsp (10 g) baking powder

½ tsp baking soda

½ tsp salt

¾ cup (170 g) unsalted butter, at room temperature

¼ cup (60 ml) vegetable oil

1⅔ cups (332 g) granulated sugar

3 large eggs, at room temperature

½ cup (120 g) sour cream, at room temperature

2 tsp (10 ml) pure vanilla extract

1 cup (240 ml) whole milk, at room temperature

MAKE THE GRAHAM CRACKER CAKE

1. Preheat the oven to 350°F (177°C). Prepare three 6-inch (15-cm) or two 8-inch (20-cm) round cake pans by spraying the sides with baking spray and fitting a parchment paper circle to the bottom of each pan.

2. Place the graham cracker crumbs in a medium bowl, and then add the flour, baking powder, baking soda and salt. Whisk the ingredients to combine them. Set the graham cracker mixture aside.

3. In the bowl of a stand mixer fitted with the paddle attachment, beat the butter at high speed for 2 minutes, until it is light and creamy. Add the oil and granulated sugar, then mix the ingredients at medium-high speed for 2 minutes. Scrape the bowl and paddle and decrease the mixer's speed to low. Add the eggs one at a time, mixing until the ingredients are well combined. Add the sour cream and vanilla and mix the ingredients at high speed for 1 minute, scraping the bowl and paddle afterward.

4. With the mixer running at low speed, add the graham cracker mixture all at once and mix the ingredients until they are just combined. Add the milk slowly and mix the ingredients until they are just incorporated. Scrape down the sides and bottom of the bowl, and stir the batter a few times to make sure there are no lumps. The batter will be thick.

5. Divide the batter between the prepared cake pans. Bake the cakes for 30 to 35 minutes. They're done when they spring back to the touch and a toothpick inserted into the centers comes out clean. Let the cakes cool in their pans for 5 minutes, then remove them from the pans and allow them to cool completely on a wire rack.

(continued)

TOASTED MARSHMALLOW BUTTERCREAM FILLING

6 large marshmallows

1 cup (226 g) unsalted butter, at room temperature

3 cups (360 g) powdered sugar

2 tsp (10 ml) pure vanilla extract

3½ oz (98 g) marshmallow crème

¼ tsp salt

CHOCOLATE BUTTERCREAM

1 batch Chocolate Buttercream (page 132)

TOPPING

½ cup (52 g) graham cracker crumbs

1 batch Marshmallow Meringue (page 140; see Notes)

NOTES

You can find my original s'mores cake at sugarandsparrow.com/smores-cake-recipe.

Remember that the Marshmallow Meringue cannot be made ahead of time. Be sure to make it right before you plan on decorating with it.

MAKE THE TOASTED MARSHMALLOW BUTTERCREAM FILLING

1. Line a medium baking sheet with parchment paper and lightly spray the surface of the parchment paper with baking spray. Place the marshmallows on the prepared baking sheet and place it on the center rack of the oven. Broil the marshmallows on high, watching them closely, until they start to brown on top. Flip them over so they can brown on the bottom as well. When both sides are well toasted, remove the marshmallows from the oven and allow them to cool to room temperature on the baking sheet.

2. In the bowl of a stand mixer fitted with the paddle attachment, beat the butter at high speed for about 5 minutes, until it is creamy and light in color. Decrease the mixer's speed to low and add the powdered sugar 2 cups (240 g) at a time, scraping the bowl and paddle after each addition. Add the vanilla, marshmallow crème, toasted marshmallows and salt. Mix the ingredients together at low speed until they are fully combined.

MAKE THE CHOCOLATE BUTTERCREAM

1. Make 1 batch of Chocolate Buttercream (page 132). Set the frosting aside.

ASSEMBLE THE CAKE

1. Level the cooled cake layers to your desired height (page 31). Fill and stack the cake layers (page 32) with Toasted Marshmallow Buttercream Filling, then crumb coat the cake (page 37) with Chocolate Buttercream. Chill the crumb-coated cake in the refrigerator for at least 30 minutes to allow the frosting to firm up.

2. Follow the Smooth Buttercream Tutorial (page 61) to create a smooth finish with Chocolate Buttercream. To begin topping the cake, apply the graham cracker crumbs all around the bottom third of the cake. Refrigerate the cake while you make the Marshmallow Meringue (page 140).

3. Fit one piping bag with a Wilton tip 1M and one piping bag with a Wilton tip 4B. Fill each piping bag with Marshmallow Meringue. Pipe rosettes and stars (page 113) in random clusters all over the cake. Carefully toast each Marshmallow Meringue cluster with a kitchen torch.

Rainbow-Striped Milk & Cereal Cake

Yield: 1 triple-layer 6-inch (15-cm) cake or 1 double-layer 8-inch (20-cm) cake
Prep time: 1 hour 5 minutes   **Bake time:** 30–35 minutes

This cake is packed with all the flavors that pair wonderfully with Saturday-morning cartoons: layers of cereal-flavored cake and buttercream infused with Cereal Milk and studded with colorful Lucky Charms marshmallows. Add some rainbow-striped buttercream (page 87) and a rainbow rope border (page 116), and you'll have the most magical cake ever! It's the perfect cake for cereal lovers of all ages and can be made with any kind of cereal you want—just substitute an equal amount of your favorite cereal to customize the flavor. I love making this cake with Froot Loops®, Fruity PEBBLES™, Cap'n Crunch® and Cinnamon Toast Crunch!

CEREAL MILK

1½ cups (54 g) Lucky Charms cereal

1½ cups (360 ml) whole milk

MILK & CEREAL CAKE

1⅔ cups (60 g) Lucky Charms cereal, marshmallows removed

2½ cups (265 g) sifted cake flour

2 tsp (10 g) baking powder

½ tsp baking soda

½ tsp salt

¾ cup (170 g) unsalted butter, at room temperature

¼ cup (60 ml) vegetable oil

1½ cups (300 g) granulated sugar

3 large eggs, at room temperature

½ cup (120 g) sour cream, at room temperature

1 tbsp (15 ml) pure vanilla extract

1 cup (240 ml) Cereal Milk, at room temperature

NOTE

You'll end up with about ¾ cup (60 g) of cereal powder after grinding the cereal.

MAKE THE CEREAL MILK

1. Place the Lucky Charms cereal in a medium bowl. Pour the milk over the cereal and let the cereal soak in the milk for 15 minutes. Strain out and discard the cereal and reserve the milk to use in the cake and buttercream recipes.

MAKE THE MILK & CEREAL CAKE

1. Preheat the oven to 350°F (177°C). Prepare three 6-inch (15-cm) or two 8-inch (20-cm) round cake pans by spraying the sides with baking spray and fitting a parchment paper circle to the bottom of each pan.

2. Grind the Lucky Charms cereal in a food processor to the consistency of a fine powder (see Note), then place it in a medium bowl. Add the sifted flour, baking powder, baking soda and salt. Whisk the ingredients to combine them, and then set the cereal-flour mixture aside.

3. In the bowl of a stand mixer fitted with the paddle attachment, beat the butter at high speed for 2 minutes, until it is light and creamy. Add the oil and granulated sugar, then mix the ingredients at medium-high speed for 2 minutes, scraping the bowl and paddle once at the halfway point. Decrease the mixer's speed to low and add the eggs one at a time, mixing just until the last egg is well combined. Add the sour cream and vanilla and mix the ingredients at high speed for 1 minute. Scrape the bowl and paddle once more.

(continued)

CEREAL MILK BUTTERCREAM

2½ cups (565 g) unsalted butter, at room temperature (see Note)

10½ cups (1.3 kg) powdered sugar

6 tbsp (90 ml) Cereal Milk, at room temperature

1½ tbsp (23 ml) pure vanilla extract

¼ tsp salt, or as needed

FILLING & TOPPING

1 cup (36 g) Lucky Charms marshmallows, divided

NOTE

The reason why this recipe yields so much buttercream is to make sure you have enough for creating the rainbow stripes and rainbow rope border. If you'd rather make just enough to fill and frost the cake, you can halve the buttercream portion of the recipe.

4. Turn the mixer off and add the cereal-flour mixture all at once. Start the mixer at low speed. Mix the ingredients until they are just combined, then add the Cereal Milk in a steady stream. Mix the ingredients until they are just incorporated. Scrape the sides and bottom of the bowl and stir the batter a few times to make sure there are no lumps. The batter will be slightly thick.

5. Divide the batter between the prepared cake pans. Bake the cakes for 30 to 35 minutes. They're done when they spring back to the touch and a toothpick inserted into the centers comes out clean. Let the cakes cool in their pans for 5 minutes, then remove them from the pans and allow them to cool completely on a wire rack.

MAKE THE CEREAL MILK BUTTERCREAM

1. In the bowl of a stand mixer fitted with the paddle attachment, beat the butter at high speed for 7 minutes, until it is fluffy and almost white in color, scraping the bowl and paddle a few times during this process.

2. Decrease the mixer's speed to low and add the powdered sugar 2 cups (240 g) at a time, scraping the bowl and paddle after each addition. Add the Cereal Milk, vanilla and salt and mix the ingredients at low speed for 1 to 2 minutes, until the ingredients are fully incorporated and the frosting is smooth.

ASSEMBLE THE CAKE

1. Level the cooled cake layers to your desired height (page 31). Fill and stack the cake layers (page 32) with a layer of Cereal Milk Buttercream, sprinkling each layer of buttercream filling with ¼ cup (9 g) of the Lucky Charms marshmallows. Crumb coat the cake (page 37) with Cereal Milk Buttercream. Chill the crumb-coated cake in the refrigerator for at least 30 minutes to allow the frosting to firm up.

2. Reserve 2 cups (430 g) of the Cereal Milk Buttercream for the rope border.

3. Use the remaining Cereal Milk Buttercream to follow the Striped Buttercream Tutorial (page 88) in order to create a rainbow-striped finish. Begin the tutorial with uncolored Cereal Milk Buttercream, then, after using the cake comb to create the grooves, divide the remaining buttercream equally among six bowls.

(continued)

AmeriColor Soft Gel Paste in Soft Pink

AmeriColor Soft Gel Paste in Lemon Yellow

AmeriColor Soft Gel Paste in Sky Blue

A

B

C

D

4. To create a rainbow-stripe color palette, use the food coloring gels and the bowls of buttercream from step 3 to make pink, orange, yellow, green, blue and purple buttercream: Add 2 drops of AmeriColor Soft Pink to the first bowl to make pink; add 1 drop of Soft Pink and 1 drop of Lemon Yellow to the second bowl to make orange; add 2 drops of Lemon Yellow to the third bowl to make yellow; add 1 drop of Lemon Yellow and 1 very small drop of Sky Blue to the fourth bowl to make green; add 1 drop of Sky Blue to the fifth bowl to make blue; and add 1 drop of Soft Pink and 1 very small drop of Sky Blue to the sixth bowl to make purple. Mix the food coloring into each of the bowls separately with a clean spoon.

5. Place each of the rainbow colors into separate piping bags and use them to fill in the grooves and complete the Striped Buttercream Tutorial (page 88).

6. While the buttercream stripes are still sticky, place ¼ cup (9 g) Lucky Charms marshmallows a few inches apart all over the sides of the cake.

7. To create the rope border, divide the 2 cups (430 g) of reserved Cereal Milk Buttercream among four bowls. Use the same food coloring gel ratios from step 4 to create pink, yellow, blue and purple buttercream. Place each buttercream color in a separate piping bag and use clean scissors to snip off a ½-inch (1.3-cm) opening on each bag.

8. Cut a 10-inch (25-cm) piece of plastic wrap and lay it out on a flat surface. Pipe each buttercream color in a straight line onto the plastic wrap with the colors directly next to one another in this order: pink, yellow, blue, purple (A). Roll up the plastic wrap so that the pink and purple buttercream meet (B), and then snip off an opening on the end of the plastic wrap.

9. Prepare a piping bag with a Wilton tip 1M and place the plastic-wrapped buttercream in it with the open side toward the piping tip (C).

10. Use the tutorial on page 116 to create a rope border around the top edge of the cake with the rainbow buttercream (D). Sprinkle the remaining Lucky Charms marshmallows on the rainbow rope border.

Almond Joy Cake

Yield: 1 triple-layer 6-inch (15-cm) cake or 1 double-layer 8-inch (20-cm) cake
Prep time: 55 minutes   **Bake time:** 40–45 minutes

I'm not normally a candy bar connoisseur, but around Halloween every year I find myself hoarding tiny Almond Joy candy bars like there's no tomorrow. The sweet coconut paired with milk chocolate and that hint of almond is irresistible to me. This recipe is fully inspired by my seasonal Almond Joy obsession and hits the spot year round. It has layers of moist yet fluffy Coconut Cake, Coconut-Almond Buttercream and beautiful chocolate ganache. If you're excited reading this description, you're going to love this cake!

COCONUT CAKE

3 cups (318 g) sifted cake flour

2 tsp (10 g) baking powder

½ tsp baking soda

1 tsp salt

1 cup (226 g) unsalted butter, at room temperature

1½ cups (300 g) granulated sugar

5 large egg whites, at room temperature

⅓ cup (80 g) sour cream, at room temperature

2 tsp (10 ml) pure vanilla extract

1 tsp coconut extract

1 cup (240 ml) canned full-fat coconut milk, at room temperature

1 cup (78 g) shredded sweetened coconut

MAKE THE COCONUT CAKE

1. Preheat the oven to 350°F (177°C). Prepare three 6-inch (15-cm) or two 8-inch (20-cm) round cake pans by spraying the sides with baking spray and fitting a parchment paper circle to the bottom of each pan.

2. In a medium bowl, whisk together the flour, baking powder, baking soda and salt. Set the flour mixture aside.

3. In the bowl of a stand mixer fitted with the paddle attachment, beat the butter at high speed for 2 minutes, until it is light and creamy. Add the granulated sugar and mix the ingredients at medium-high speed for 2 minutes, scraping the bowl and paddle as needed. Decrease the mixer's speed to low and add the egg whites one at a time, mixing the ingredients until they are well combined. Add the sour cream, vanilla and coconut extract and mix the ingredients at high speed for 1 minute. Scrape the bowl and paddle once more. The mixture will look curdled at this point, but it will look like smooth cake batter by the end.

4. With the mixer running at low speed, add the flour mixture all at once. When the flour mixture is just beginning to combine with the butter-sugar mixture, add the coconut milk in a slow, steady stream. Mix the ingredients at low speed until they are incorporated. Scrape the sides and bottom of the bowl and stir the batter by hand a few times to make sure there are no large lumps, then gently fold in the shredded coconut.

5. Divide the batter evenly between the prepared cake pans. Bake the cakes for 40 to 45 minutes. They're done when they spring back to the touch and a toothpick inserted into the centers comes out clean. Let the cakes cool in their pans for 5 minutes, then remove them from the pans and allow them to cool completely on a wire rack.

(continued)

Almond Joy Cake *(continued)*

COCONUT-ALMOND BUTTERCREAM

2½ cups (565 g) unsalted butter, at room temperature

10½ cups (1.3 kg) powdered sugar

1¼ tsp (6 ml) pure vanilla extract

1¼ tsp (6 ml) pure almond extract

2½ tsp (13 ml) coconut extract

4 tbsp (60 ml) whole milk, at room temperature

¼ tsp salt, or as needed

TOPPING

1 batch Chocolate Ganache Drip (page 135)

½ cup (50 g) toasted sliced almonds

MAKE THE COCONUT-ALMOND BUTTERCREAM

1. In the bowl of a stand mixer fitted with the paddle attachment, beat the butter at medium-high speed for about 7 minutes, until it is creamy and almost white in color.

2. Decrease the mixer's speed to low and add the powdered sugar 2 cups (240 g) at a time, scraping the bowl and paddle after each addition. Add the vanilla, almond extract, coconut extract, milk and salt. Mix the ingredients at low speed for 1 to 2 minutes, until they are fully incorporated.

MAKE THE CHOCOLATE GANACHE DRIP

1. Make 1 batch of Chocolate Ganache Drip (page 135). Allow the ganache to cool to room temperature.

ASSEMBLE THE CAKE

1. Level the cooled cake layers to your desired height (page 31). Fill and stack the cake using the method for soft fillings (page 35): Use Coconut-Almond Buttercream as the dam, spread a ¼-inch (6-mm)-thick layer of ganache inside the buttercream dam, then top the ganache with more Coconut-Almond Buttercream, being careful to stay within the buttercream dam. Repeat the filling and stacking process for the remaining layers until you have one cake layer remaining, then place that final cake layer on top, upside down, so that the bottom of that layer becomes the top of the cake.

2. Crumb coat the cake (page 37) with Coconut-Almond Buttercream. Chill the crumb-coated cake in the refrigerator for at least 30 minutes to allow the frosting to firm up.

3. Set aside 1½ cups (323 g) of Coconut-Almond Buttercream for the rope border. Use the remaining buttercream to create a combed texture finish (page 82). Add the toasted almonds to the bottom third of the cake while the frosting is still sticky, reserving some for the top of the cake.

4. Gently heat the remaining ganache back to drip consistency (page 98) and create a curtain drip (page 102). When you've finished dripping the cake, place it back in the refrigerator for at least 5 minutes to let the drip set up.

5. With the reserved Coconut-Almond Buttercream, create a rope border (page 116) using a Wilton tip 1M. Sprinkle the remaining toasted almonds on top of the rope border.

Lemon-Raspberry Painterly Cake

Yield: 1 triple-layer 6-inch (15-cm) cake or 1 double-layer 8-inch (20-cm) cake
Prep time: 1 hour 10 minutes   **Bake time:** 28–32 minutes

This pretty cake is melt-in-your-mouth delicious and perfect for celebrating anything—even if your cause for celebration is just a warm spring day! The colors on the outside are perfect for representing the bright and refreshing flavors inside: layers of extra soft and zesty lemon cake paired with my favorite Raspberry Buttercream. The best thing about this painterly finish is that it looks complex, yet it's incredibly easy to create. For best results, read about buttercream color theory on page 55 to mix the perfect color palette, and use the tutorial on page 73 to get the painterly technique down.

LEMON CAKE

2½ cups (265 g) sifted cake flour

1 tbsp (15 g) baking powder

½ tsp salt

1½ cups (300 g) granulated sugar

1 tbsp (6 g) grated lemon zest (about 1 medium lemon)

½ cup (113 g) unsalted butter, at room temperature

4 large egg whites, at room temperature

½ cup (120 ml) vegetable oil

½ tsp pure lemon extract

1¼ cups (300 ml) full-fat buttermilk, at room temperature

MAKE THE LEMON CAKE

1. Preheat the oven to 350°F (177°C). Prepare three 6-inch (15-cm) or two 8-inch (20-cm) round cake pans by spraying the sides with baking spray and fitting a parchment paper circle to the bottom of each pan.

2. In a medium bowl, combine the flour, baking powder and salt. Whisk the ingredients to combine them, and then set the bowl aside.

3. In the bowl of a stand mixer fitted with the paddle attachment, mix together the granulated sugar and lemon zest at low speed for about 1 minute, until the mixture is fragrant and the sugar and zest are well combined. Add the butter and cream it together with the lemon-sugar mixture at medium speed for 2 to 3 minutes, until the mixture is light and fluffy. Decrease the mixer's speed to low and add the egg whites, one at a time, mixing until they are just combined and scraping the bowl and paddle as needed. Add the vegetable oil and lemon extract, increase the mixer's speed to high and beat the ingredients for 1 minute.

4. Turn the mixer off and add the flour mixture all at once. Start the mixer at low speed. Mix until the ingredients are just combined, and then, with the mixer still running, slowly pour in the buttermilk. Mix the ingredients at low speed for about 30 seconds, until they are just combined. Scrape the sides and bottom of the bowl and stir the batter with a whisk a few times to make sure there are no lumps.

5. Divide the batter evenly between the prepared cake pans. Bake the cakes for 28 to 32 minutes. They're done when they spring back to the touch and a toothpick inserted into the centers comes out clean or with just a few moist crumbs on it. Let the cakes cool in their pans for 5 minutes, then remove them from the pans and allow them to cool completely on a wire rack.

(continued)

RASPBERRY BUTTERCREAM

1 cup (17 g) freeze-dried raspberries (see Note)

1 cup (226 g) unsalted butter, at room temperature

3 tbsp (45 ml) whole milk, at room temperature

1 tsp pure vanilla extract

3½ cups (420 g) powdered sugar

¼ tsp salt

LEMON BUTTERCREAM

1 cup (226 g) unsalted butter, at room temperature

3½ cups (420 g) powdered sugar

2 tbsp (30 ml) fresh lemon juice, at room temperature (about 1 small lemon)

2 tsp (10 ml) whole milk, at room temperature

¼ tsp salt, or as needed

MAKE THE RASPBERRY BUTTERCREAM

1. With a food processor, grind the raspberries into a fine powder. Sift out the seeds (if a few seeds end up in the powder, that is okay). Set the raspberry powder aside.

2. In the bowl of a stand mixer fitted with the paddle attachment, beat the butter at high speed for about 5 minutes, until it is creamy and light in color. Add the milk, vanilla and raspberry powder. Mix the ingredients at medium speed, scraping the bowl and paddle as needed, until they are well combined.

3. Decrease the mixer's speed to low and add the powdered sugar 2 cups (240 g) at a time, scraping the bowl and paddle after each addition. Add the salt and mix the ingredients at low speed for about 1 minute, until the ingredients are well incorporated and the frosting is smooth. Leave the buttercream uncolored for now and set it aside.

MAKE THE LEMON BUTTERCREAM

1. In the bowl of a stand mixer fitted with the paddle attachment, beat the butter at high speed for about 7 minutes, until it is creamy and almost white in color.

2. Decrease the mixer's speed to low and add the powdered sugar 2 cups (240 g) at a time, scraping the bowl and paddle after each addition.

3. Add the lemon juice, milk and salt and mix the ingredients at low speed for 1 to 2 minutes, until the ingredients are well incorporated and the frosting is smooth. Leave the buttercream uncolored for now and set it aside.

NOTE

Freeze-dried raspberries are not the same as frozen raspberries. The process of freeze-drying removes all of the liquid from the berries and amplifies their flavor, making them perfect for flavoring buttercream without altering its consistency. Look for them near the dried fruits in your local grocery store.

AmeriColor Soft Gel Paste in Fuchsia

AmeriColor Soft Gel Paste in Electric Pink

AmeriColor Soft Gel Paste in Lemon Yellow

ASSEMBLE THE CAKE

1. Level the cooled cake layers to your desired height (page 31). Reserve ½ cup (108 g) of the Raspberry Buttercream, then fill and stack the cake layers (page 32) with the remaining Raspberry Buttercream.

2. Crumb coat the cake (page 37) with Lemon Buttercream. Don't worry about the different buttercream colors mixing in the crumb coat—the color mixture will be covered up in the following steps. Chill the crumb-coated cake in the refrigerator for at least 30 minutes to allow the frosting to firm up.

3. Frost a smooth buttercream finish with Lemon Buttercream using the tutorial on page 62, then chill the cake in the refrigerator for at least 20 minutes while you mix the buttercream colors in the next step.

4. Mix the buttercream color palette: Place ⅓ cup (72 g) of the Lemon Buttercream in a small bowl. In a second small bowl, create a light pink color by mixing 3 to 4 teaspoons (12 to 16 g) of the reserved Raspberry Buttercream with about ⅛ cup (27 g) of the Lemon Buttercream. Divide the remaining Raspberry Buttercream between a third and fourth small bowl. Tint the third bowl a deeper raspberry color using 3 drops of Ameri-Color Fuchsia and 2 drops of AmeriColor Electric Pink. Tint the fourth bowl a medium-pink color using 2 drops AmeriColor Electric Pink and 1 drop AmeriColor Fuchsia. Tint the bowl of uncolored Lemon Buttercream with 3 drops of AmeriColor Lemon Yellow to create a deeper yellow color.

5. Follow the tutorial on page 74 to create a painterly finish using the buttercream color palette you created in step 4.

Ferrero Rocher® Cake with Nutella® Ganache Drip

Yield: 1 triple-layer 6-inch (15-cm) cake or 1 double-layer 8-inch (20-cm) cake
Prep time: 50 minutes   **Bake time:** 32–36 minutes

Chocolate and hazelnut were just meant to be together. This recipe is for all those who find this flavor pairing completely irresistible: layers of rich chocolate cake paired beautifully with Nutella-infused buttercream and topped with Nutella ganache, chopped toasted hazelnuts and Ferrero Rocher chocolates. It's everything you could ever want in a chocolate-hazelnut cake! This recipe is the perfect opportunity to practice smoothing buttercream, dripping a cake and piping buttercream swirls.

CHOCOLATE CAKE

2 cups (266 g) all-purpose flour

1⅔ cups (332 g) granulated sugar

⅔ cup (60 g) natural unsweetened cocoa powder

2 tsp (10 g) baking soda

1 tsp baking powder

½ tsp salt

½ cup (120 ml) vegetable oil

2 large eggs, at room temperature

1½ tsp (8 ml) pure vanilla extract

1 cup (240 ml) full-fat buttermilk, at room temperature

1 cup (240 ml) hot coffee or hot water

NUTELLA® BUTTERCREAM

1½ cups (339 g) unsalted butter, at room temperature

5¼ cups (630 g) powdered sugar

¾ cup (225 g) Nutella hazelnut spread

1 tbsp (15 ml) pure vanilla extract

2 tbsp (30 ml) whole milk, at room temperature

¼ tsp salt

MAKE THE CHOCOLATE CAKE

1. Preheat the oven to 350°F (177°C). Prepare three 6-inch (15-cm) or two 8-inch (20-cm) round cake pans by spraying the sides with baking spray and fitting a parchment paper circle to the bottom of each pan.

2. In the bowl of a stand mixer fitted with the paddle attachment, combine the flour, granulated sugar, cocoa powder, baking soda, baking powder and salt. Mix the ingredients at low speed for 30 seconds to fully combine them. Add the oil, eggs, vanilla and buttermilk and mix the ingredients together at low speed until they are just combined. With the mixer still running at low speed, add the hot coffee or water in a slow stream. Mix the ingredients at low speed for 1 minute, until they are fully combined. The batter will be thin.

3. Divide the batter evenly between the prepared cake pans. Bake the cakes for 32 to 36 minutes, until a toothpick inserted into the centers comes out clean. Let the cakes cool in their pans for 5 minutes, then remove them from the pans and allow them to cool completely on a wire rack.

MAKE THE NUTELLA® BUTTERCREAM

1. In the bowl of a stand mixer fitted with the paddle attachment, beat the butter at medium-high speed for about 5 minutes, until it is creamy and light in color.

2. Decrease the mixer's speed to low and add the powdered sugar 2 cups (240 g) at a time, scraping the bowl and paddle after each addition and making sure each addition is fully incorporated before adding the next. Add the Nutella, vanilla, milk and salt and mix the ingredients at low speed for 2 minutes, until the frosting is smooth.

(continued)

NUTELLA® GANACHE DRIP

½ cup (150 g) Nutella hazelnut spread

⅓ cup (80 ml) heavy cream

ADDITIONAL TOPPINGS & FILLINGS

6 Ferrero Rocher chocolates, roughly chopped

½ cup (65 g) toasted roughly chopped hazelnuts

6 Ferrero Rocher chocolates, whole

MAKE THE NUTELLA® GANACHE DRIP

1. Place the Nutella in a small glass or stainless steel bowl and set it aside. In a small saucepan over medium-high heat, warm the cream, stirring it constantly with a whisk, until it begins to simmer.

2. When the cream reaches a simmer, remove the saucepan from the heat and pour the cream over the Nutella. Let the mixture sit for about 30 seconds, and then whisk the Nutella and cream together until the consistency is uniform and smooth.

ASSEMBLE THE CAKE

1. Level the cooled cake layers to your desired height (page 31). Place the first cake layer on a turntable and top the cake layer with about ¾ cup (161 g) of the Nutella Buttercream. Sprinkle a layer of chopped Ferrero Rocher chocolates on top of the Nutella Buttercream, then add the second cake layer, and repeat the filling process with any additional layers until you have one cake layer remaining. Place the final cake layer on top, upside down, so that the bottom of the layer becomes the top of the cake.

2. Crumb coat the cake (page 37) with Nutella Buttercream. Chill the crumb-coated cake in the refrigerator for at least 30 minutes to allow the frosting to firm up.

3. Follow the Combed Texture Tutorial (page 82) to create a textured finish with the Nutella Buttercream. Apply the hazelnuts to the bottom third of the cake. Refrigerate the cake for at least 20 minutes.

4. Create a curtain drip (page 102) with the Nutella Ganache Drip, then refrigerate the cake for 5 minutes to let the drip set up. Meanwhile, fit a piping bag with a Wilton tip 1M and fill it with the remaining Nutella Buttercream.

5. Pipe a swirl border (page 116) along the top of the cake, spacing the swirls about 1 inch (2.5 cm) apart. Place the whole Ferrero Rocher chocolates in the spaces between each swirl, then sprinkle each swirl with hazelnuts.

Raspberry-Almond Impressionist Cake

Yield: 1 triple-layer 6-inch (15-cm) cake or 1 double-layer 8-inch (20-cm) cake
Prep time: 1 hour   **Bake time:** 28–32 minutes

One of my first painterly buttercream finishes was this spatula-painted technique, mostly inspired by the impressionist art I'd seen at a van Gogh exhibit. I couldn't help but stare at the paintings and see buttercream instead of oil paints. To my delight, I found that buttercream is the perfect medium to paint with! For this cake, you'll be using two different flavors of buttercream—raspberry and almond—to create a spatula-painted masterpiece atop layers of deliciously soft and moist Almond Cake paired beautifully with Raspberry Buttercream. Your cake will taste just as beautiful as it looks!

ALMOND CAKE

2½ cups (265 g) sifted cake flour

2 tsp (10 g) baking powder

½ tsp baking soda

½ tsp salt

½ cup (113 g) unsalted butter, at room temperature

1½ cups (300 g) granulated sugar

4 large egg whites, at room temperature

½ cup (120 ml) vegetable oil

2 tsp (10 ml) pure almond extract

1 tsp pure vanilla extract

1¼ cups (300 ml) full-fat buttermilk, at room temperature

MAKE THE ALMOND CAKE

1. Preheat the oven to 350°F (177°C). Prepare three 6-inch (15-cm) or two 8-inch (20-cm) round cake pans by spraying the sides with baking spray and fitting a parchment paper circle to the bottom of each pan.

2. In a medium bowl, combine the flour, baking powder, baking soda and salt. Whisk the ingredients to combine them, and then set the bowl aside.

3. In the bowl of a stand mixer fitted with the paddle attachment, beat the butter at high speed for about 2 minutes, until it is creamy. Add the sugar and mix the ingredients at medium-high speed for 2 minutes, scraping the bowl and paddle at the halfway point. Decrease the mixer's speed to low and add the egg whites, one at a time, mixing until they are just combined and scraping the bowl and paddle as needed. Add the vegetable oil, almond extract and vanilla, increase the mixer's speed to high and beat the ingredients for 1 minute.

4. Turn the mixer off and add the flour mixture all at once. Start the mixer at low speed. Mix until the ingredients are just combined, and then, with the mixer still running, slowly pour in the buttermilk. Mix the ingredients at low speed for about 30 seconds, until they are just combined. Scrape the sides and bottom of the bowl and stir the batter with a whisk a few times to make sure there are no lumps.

5. Divide the batter evenly between the prepared cake pans. Bake the cakes for 28 to 32 minutes. They're done when they spring back to the touch and a toothpick inserted into the centers comes out clean or with just a few moist crumbs on it. Let the cakes cool in their pans for 5 minutes, then remove them from the pans and allow them to cool completely on a wire rack.

(continued)

Raspberry-Almond Impressionist Cake *(continued)*

(continued)

RASPBERRY BUTTERCREAM

1 cup (17 g) freeze-dried raspberries (see Note)

1 cup (226 g) unsalted butter, at room temperature

3 tbsp (45 ml) whole milk, at room temperature

1 tsp pure vanilla extract

3½ cups (420 g) powdered sugar

Pinch of salt

ALMOND BUTTERCREAM

1 cup (226 g) unsalted butter, at room temperature

3½ cups (420 g) powdered sugar

1 tsp pure almond extract

1 tsp pure vanilla extract

2 tbsp (30 ml) whole milk, at room temperature

¼ tsp salt, or as needed

MAKE THE RASPBERRY BUTTERCREAM

1. With a food processor, grind the raspberries into a fine powder. Sift out as many seeds as you can. Set the raspberry powder aside.

2. In the bowl of a stand mixer fitted with the paddle attachment, beat the butter at high speed for about 5 minutes, scraping the bowl and paddle as needed, until it is creamy and light in color. Add the milk, vanilla and raspberry powder and mix the ingredients at medium speed for 3 minutes.

3. Decrease the mixer's speed to low and add the powdered sugar 1 cup (120 g) at a time, scraping the bowl and paddle after each addition. Add the salt and mix the ingredients for 1 minute, until the buttercream is uniform and smooth.

MAKE THE ALMOND BUTTERCREAM

1. In a stand mixer fitted with the paddle attachment, beat the butter at medium-high speed for about 7 minutes, until it is creamy and almost white in color.

2. Decrease the mixer's speed to low and add the powdered sugar 2 cups (240 g) at a time, scraping the bowl and paddle after each addition.

3. Add the almond extract, vanilla, milk and salt and mix the ingredients at low speed for 1 to 2 minutes, until the ingredients are fully incorporated and the frosting is smooth.

ASSEMBLE THE CAKE

1. Level the cooled cake layers to your desired height (page 31). Reserve ¼ cup (54 g) of the Raspberry Buttercream, then fill and stack the cake layers (page 32) with the remaining Raspberry Buttercream.

2. Crumb coat the cake (page 37) with Almond Buttercream. Don't worry about the different buttercream colors mixing in the crumb coat—the color mixture will be covered up in the following steps. Chill the crumb-coated cake in the refrigerator for at least 30 minutes to allow the frosting to firm up.

3. Frost a smooth buttercream finish (page 61) with Almond Buttercream, then chill the cake in the refrigerator for at least 20 minutes while you mix the buttercream colors in the next step.

(continued)

FOOD COLORING GELS

AmeriColor Soft Gel Paste in Soft Pink

AmeriColor Soft Gel Paste in Peach

AmeriColor Soft Gel Paste in Fuchsia

4. Create the buttercream color palette: Divide the remaining Almond Buttercream among 5 bowls. Add 1 to 2 teaspoons (4 to 8 g) of the Raspberry Buttercream to the first bowl to create a light pink color. Add 2 drops of AmeriColor Soft Pink to the second bowl to create a medium-pink color. Add 1 drop of AmeriColor Peach to the third bowl and 3 drops of AmeriColor Peach to the fourth bowl to create two different intensities of peach color. Add 3 drops of AmeriColor Fuchsia to the fifth bowl to create a deep fuchsia color.

5. Create an impressionist finish using the tutorial on page 70 and the buttercream color palette you created in step 4.

NOTE

Freeze-dried raspberries are not the same as frozen raspberries. The process of freeze-drying removes all of the liquid from the berries and amplifies their flavor, making them perfect for flavoring buttercream without altering its consistency.

Mint Chocolate Chip Cake

Yield: 1 triple-layer 6-inch (15-cm) cake or 1 double-layer 8-inch (20-cm) cake
Prep time: 50 minutes   **Bake time:** 32–36 minutes

This minty, chocolatey cake is a real stunner and hits the spot for any mint chocolate lover! Reminiscent of the classic ice cream flavor, this cake features layers of mint-infused chocolate cake, buttercream studded with chocolate chips and a glorious coating of chocolate ganache spilling over the edges. To make the buttercream easy to work with, be sure to chop the chocolate chips as finely as you can before adding them to the frosting. If you find that the chocolate chip pieces are dragging too much through the buttercream while you're trying to smooth the cake, complete step 6 in the tutorial on page 62 for an easy troubleshooting tip.

MINT CHOCOLATE CAKE

2 cups (266 g) all-purpose flour

1⅔ cups (332 g) granulated sugar

⅔ cup (60 g) natural unsweetened cocoa powder

2 tsp (10 g) baking soda

1 tsp baking powder

½ tsp kosher salt

½ cup (120 ml) vegetable oil

2 large eggs, at room temperature

1 tsp pure vanilla extract

½ tsp pure peppermint extract

1 cup (240 ml) full-fat buttermilk, at room temperature

1 cup (240 ml) hot water

MAKE THE MINT CHOCOLATE CAKE

1. Preheat the oven to 350°F (177°C). Prepare three 6-inch (15-cm) or two 8-inch (20-cm) round cake pans by spraying the sides with baking spray and fitting a parchment paper circle to the bottom of each pan.

2. In the bowl of a stand mixer fitted with the paddle attachment, combine the flour, granulated sugar, cocoa powder, baking soda, baking powder and kosher salt. Stir the ingredients together at low speed for 30 seconds to fully combine them. Add the oil, eggs, vanilla, peppermint extract and buttermilk and mix the ingredients at low speed until they are just combined. With the mixer still running at low speed, add the hot water in a slow stream, then increase the mixer's speed to medium and beat the mixture for about 2 minutes, until it is smooth. The batter will be very thin.

3. Divide the batter evenly between the prepared cake pans, making sure each pan is no more than two-thirds full. Bake the cakes for 32 to 36 minutes, until a toothpick inserted into the centers comes out clean. Let the cakes cool in their pans for 5 minutes, then remove them from the pans and allow them to cool completely on a wire rack.

(continued)

Mint Chocolate Chip Cake *(continued)*

MINT CHOCOLATE CHIP BUTTERCREAM

2 cups (452 g) unsalted butter, at room temperature

7 cups (840 g) powdered sugar

6 tbsp (90 ml) heavy cream

2 tsp (10 ml) pure vanilla extract

1 tsp pure peppermint extract

¼ tsp salt

2–3 drops AmeriColor Soft Gel Paste in Mint Green

½ cup (93 g) semisweet chocolate chips, finely chopped

TOPPING

1 batch Chocolate Ganache Drip (page 135)

MAKE THE MINT CHOCOLATE CHIP BUTTERCREAM

1. In the bowl of a stand mixer fitted with the paddle attachment, beat the butter at medium-high speed for about 7 minutes, until it is creamy and almost white in color.

2. Decrease the mixer's speed to low and add the powdered sugar 2 cups (240 g) at a time, scraping the bowl and paddle after each addition to make sure it is fully incorporated before adding the next one. Add the cream, vanilla, peppermint extract and salt and mix the ingredients together at medium-low speed for 2 minutes, until they are fully incorporated.

3. Add the AmeriColor Mint Green until the desired shade of mint green is reached. Then gently fold in the chocolate chips.

MAKE THE CHOCOLATE GANACHE DRIP

1. Make 1 batch of Chocolate Ganache Drip (page 135). Set the ganache aside.

ASSEMBLE THE CAKE

1. Level the cooled cake layers to your desired height (page 31). Fill and stack the cake layers (page 32) with Mint Chocolate Chip Buttercream, then crumb coat the cake (page 37) with Mint Chocolate Chip Buttercream. Chill the crumb-coated cake in the refrigerator for at least 30 minutes to allow the frosting to firm up.

2. Reserve about 1 cup (215 g) of the Mint Chocolate Chip Buttercream for the piping on top, then create a smooth buttercream finish (page 61) with the remaining Mint Chocolate Chip Buttercream.

3. Create a curtain drip (page 102) with the Chocolate Ganache Drip. Chill the cake in the refrigerator for about 5 minutes while you fit three piping bags with Wilton tips 4B, 6B and 1A. Divide the remaining Mint Chocolate Chip Buttercream between the three piping bags. Finish the cake by piping a crescent border (page 116) of stars.

Semi-Naked Carrot Cake

Yield: 1 triple-layer 6-inch (15-cm) cake or 1 double-layer 8-inch (20-cm) cake
Prep time: 50 minutes   **Bake time:** 35–40 minutes

A true classic, this carrot cake is extra moist, has the most incredible spice flavor and is so easy to throw together. It's a very simple cake, and the only challenge is in the grating of the carrots (although that part does make for a great arm workout). The cake is paired with smooth and velvety Cream Cheese Buttercream to make it extra addicting, and it's one of those cakes that gets even better with time—preparing it a day or two ahead will make it even more moist and flavorful! To make sure you don't have crumbs peeking through your semi-naked buttercream finish, refer to page 66 for the perfect tutorial.

CARROT CAKE

2½ cups (333 g) all-purpose flour

2 tsp (10 g) baking powder

1 tsp baking soda

½ tsp salt

2 tsp (5 g) ground cinnamon

1 tsp ground nutmeg

1 tsp ground ginger

¼ tsp ground cloves

½ cup (100 g) granulated sugar

1½ cups (300 g) packed brown sugar

1 cup (240 ml) vegetable oil

4 large eggs, at room temperature

¾ cup (135 g) smooth unsweetened applesauce

1 tsp pure vanilla extract

2 cups (260 g) grated carrots (about 4 large)

CREAM CHEESE BUTTERCREAM

1 batch Cream Cheese Buttercream (page 130)

MAKE THE CARROT CAKE

1. Preheat the oven to 350°F (177°C). Prepare three 6-inch (15-cm) or two 8-inch (20-cm) round cake pans by spraying the sides with baking spray and fitting a parchment paper circle to the bottom of each pan.

2. In a medium bowl, whisk together the flour, baking powder, baking soda, salt, cinnamon, nutmeg, ginger and cloves. In a large bowl, whisk together the granulated sugar, brown sugar, oil, eggs, applesauce and vanilla.

3. Using a rubber spatula, fold the sugar mixture into the flour mixture until the two are just combined, then fold in the carrots. At this point, you can fold in any add-ins if you wish (see Notes).

4. Divide the batter evenly between the prepared cake pans. Bake the cakes for 35 to 40 minutes, or until a toothpick inserted into the centers comes out clean. Allow the cakes to cool in their pans for 10 minutes, then remove them from the pans and allow them to cool completely on a wire rack.

MAKE THE CREAM CHEESE BUTTERCREAM

1. Make 1 batch of Cream Cheese Buttercream (page 130). Set the frosting aside.

(continued)

TOPPINGS

1 batch White Chocolate Ganache Drip
(page 136)

1–2 drops AmeriColor Soft Gel Paste in
Peach

Assorted edible flowers (see Notes)

ASSEMBLE THE CAKE

1. Level the cooled cake layers to your desired height (page 31). Fill
and stack the cake layers (page 32) with Cream Cheese Buttercream, then
crumb coat the cake (page 37) with Cream Cheese Buttercream. Chill
the crumb-coated cake in the refrigerator for at least 30 minutes to allow the
frosting to firm up.

2. Frost the cake with a semi-naked finish (page 65) with the remaining
Cream Cheese Buttercream. Chill the cake for 20 minutes. In the meantime,
make the White Chocolate Ganache Drip (page 136), tinting the ganache
with the AmeriColor Peach.

3. Create a half drip (page 100) with the White Chocolate Ganache Drip,
then garnish the cake with the edible flowers.

NOTES

Try these add-in ideas: 1 cup (145 g) of raisins, ½ cup (39 g) of shredded
sweetened coconut or 2 cups (218 g) of toasted pecans.

I used fresh edible pansies, carnations and daisies from my local florist.
Be sure to ask your local florist or natural grocer for edible flower
recommendations. You can alternatively find freeze-dried edible flowers
on Etsy and Amazon.

Chocolate-Covered Strawberry Cake

Yield: 1 triple-layer 6-inch (15-cm) cake or 1 double-layer 8-inch (20-cm) cake
Prep time: 45 minutes   **Bake time:** 32–36 minutes

I can't imagine this Chocolate-Covered Strawberry Cake without the glistening chocolate ganache dripping down that beautiful strawberry-flecked buttercream. It's the perfect excuse to put your ganache drip skills into practice. Underneath that beautiful drip, you'll find layers of decadent chocolate cake and satisfying Strawberry Buttercream. This is one of the most sensual flavor combos of all (cue the sax solo), but there's no need to save this recipe for a romantic occasion. You can make it any day and have a good time!

CHOCOLATE CAKE

2 cups (266 g) all-purpose flour

1⅔ cups (332 g) granulated sugar

⅔ cup (60 g) natural unsweetened cocoa powder

2 tsp (10 g) baking soda

1 tsp baking powder

½ tsp salt

½ cup (120 ml) vegetable oil

2 large eggs, at room temperature

1½ tsp (8 ml) pure vanilla extract

1 cup (240 ml) full-fat buttermilk, at room temperature

1 cup (240 ml) hot coffee or hot water

STRAWBERRY BUTTERCREAM

2 cups (34 g) freeze-dried strawberries

2 cups (452 g) unsalted butter, at room temperature

6 tbsp (90 ml) whole milk, at room temperature

2 tsp (10 ml) pure vanilla extract

7 cups (840 g) powdered sugar

¼ tsp salt

MAKE THE CHOCOLATE CAKE

1. Preheat the oven to 350°F (177°C). Prepare three 6-inch (15-cm) or two 8-inch (20-cm) round cake pans by spraying the sides with baking spray and fitting a parchment paper circle to the bottom of each pan.

2. In the bowl of a stand mixer fitted with the paddle attachment, combine the flour, granulated sugar, cocoa powder, baking soda, baking powder and salt. Stir the ingredients together at low speed for 30 seconds to fully combine them. Add the oil, eggs, vanilla and buttermilk and mix the ingredients at low speed until they are just combined. With the mixer still running at low speed, add the hot coffee or water in a slow stream. Mix the ingredients for 1 to 2 minutes, until they are fully combined. The batter will be very thin.

3. Divide the batter evenly between the prepared cake pans. Bake the cakes for 32 to 36 minutes, until a toothpick inserted into the centers comes out clean. Let the cakes cool for 5 minutes in their pans, then remove them from the pans and allow them to cool completely on a wire rack.

MAKE THE STRAWBERRY BUTTERCREAM

1. With a food processor, grind the strawberries into a fine powder. Set the strawberry powder aside. In the bowl of a stand mixer fitted with the paddle attachment, beat the butter at medium speed for about 5 minutes, until it is creamy and light in color. Add the milk, vanilla and strawberry powder and mix the ingredients together at medium speed for 1 minute.

2. Decrease the mixer's speed to low and add the powdered sugar 2 cups (240 g) at a time, mixing well and scraping the bowl and paddle after each addition. Add the salt and mix the buttercream at low speed for 1 minute, until the frosting is smooth and well combined.

(continued)

Chocolate-Covered Strawberry Cake *(continued)*

TOPPINGS

1 batch Chocolate Ganache Drip (page 135)

Fresh strawberries dipped in Chocolate Ganache Drip, as needed

MAKE THE CHOCOLATE GANACHE DRIP

1. Make 1 batch of Chocolate Ganache Drip (page 135). Set the ganache aside.

ASSEMBLE THE CAKE

1. Level the cooled cake layers to your desired height (page 31). Fill and stack the cake layers (page 32) with Strawberry Buttercream, then crumb coat the cake (page 37) with Strawberry Buttercream. Chill the crumb-coated cake in the refrigerator for at least 30 minutes to allow the frosting to firm up.

2. Reserve about 1 cup (215 g) of the Strawberry Buttercream for the swirl border, then create a smooth buttercream finish (page 61) with the remaining Strawberry Buttercream. Chill the cake in the refrigerator for 20 minutes to allow the frosting to firm up.

3. Create a traditional drip (page 100) with the Chocolate Ganache Drip, then place the cake in the refrigerator while you prepare a piping bag with a Wilton tip 1M and fill it with the remaining Strawberry Buttercream.

4. Pipe a swirl border (page 116), spacing the swirls 1 inch (2.5 cm) apart. Place the fresh strawberries between the swirls.

Pumpkin Spice Latte Cake

Yield: 1 triple-layer 6-inch (15-cm) cake or 1 double-layer 8-inch (20-cm) cake
Prep time: 55 minutes   **Bake time:** 38–42 minutes

I start to feel autumn at a soul level as soon as the coffee shops start adding pumpkin spice lattes to their menus. The pumpkin and coffee combination is warm and inviting, and it pairs perfectly with vibrant leaves and a comfy sweater. This cake is for all who live for the magic of fall: layers of my favorite ultra-moist spiced pumpkin cake and coffee-forward buttercream, dripping with white chocolate ganache. Add some pretty piped pumpkins on top to make it even more festive—this recipe's tutorial on page 203 will show you how!

PUMPKIN SPICE CAKE

2¾ cups (292 g) sifted cake flour

2½ tsp (13 g) baking powder

1 tsp baking soda

1 tsp salt

2 tsp (5 g) ground cinnamon

1 tsp ground allspice

1 tsp ground nutmeg

½ tsp ground ginger

1 cup (226 g) unsalted butter, at room temperature

1 cup (200 g) granulated sugar

¾ cup (150 g) packed brown sugar

3 large eggs, at room temperature

2 tsp (10 ml) pure vanilla extract

1½ cups (345 g) canned pure pumpkin purée

1 cup (240 ml) full-fat buttermilk, at room temperature

MAKE THE PUMPKIN SPICE CAKE

1. Preheat the oven to 350°F (177°C). Prepare three 6-inch (15-cm) or two 8-inch (20-cm) round cake pans by spraying the sides with baking spray and fitting a parchment paper circle to the bottom of each pan.

2. In a medium bowl, whisk together the flour, baking powder, baking soda, salt, cinnamon, allspice, nutmeg and ginger. Set the flour mixture aside.

3. In the bowl of a stand mixer fitted with the paddle attachment, beat the butter at high speed for 2 minutes, until it is light and creamy. Add the granulated sugar and brown sugar and mix the ingredients together at medium-high speed for 2 minutes, scraping the bowl and paddle as needed. Decrease the mixer's speed to low and add the eggs one at a time, mixing thoroughly after each addition. Add the vanilla and pumpkin purée and mix the ingredients at medium-high speed for 1 minute, scraping the bowl and paddle once more. The batter will look very curdled at this point, but don't worry—it will transform into smooth cake batter by the end.

4. Add the flour mixture and mix the ingredients at low speed. When the flour mixture just begins to combine with the butter-sugar mixture, add the buttermilk in a steady stream and mix the ingredients until they are just incorporated. Scrape the sides and bottom of the bowl and stir the batter a few times to make sure there are no lumps. The batter will be thick.

5. Divide the batter evenly between the prepared cake pans. Bake the cakes for 38 to 42 minutes, until a toothpick inserted into the centers comes out clean. Let the cakes cool in their pans for 10 minutes, then remove the cakes from the pans and allow them to cool completely on a wire rack.

(continued)

CREAMY COFFEE BUTTERCREAM

1½ tsp (2 g) instant coffee or espresso powder

3 tbsp (45 ml) whole milk, at room temperature

2 cups (452 g) unsalted butter, at room temperature

7 cups (840 g) powdered sugar

4 tsp (20 ml) pure vanilla extract

¼ tsp salt, or as needed

TOPPINGS

½ cup (186 g) crushed Lotus Biscoff Cookies

1 batch White Chocolate Ganache Drip (page 136)

FOOD COLORING GELS

AmeriColor Soft Gel Paste in Orange

AmeriColor Soft Gel Paste in Chocolate Brown

AmeriColor Soft Gel Paste in Wedgewood

MAKE THE CREAMY COFFEE BUTTERCREAM

1. In a small bowl, combine the instant coffee or espresso powder with the milk. Set the mixture aside. In the bowl of a stand mixer fitted with the paddle attachment, beat the butter at medium-high speed for about 5 minutes, scraping the bowl and paddle occasionally, until it is light and fluffy.

2. Decrease the mixer's speed to low and add the powdered sugar 2 cups (240 g) at a time, scraping the bowl and paddle after each addition. Add the vanilla, coffee-milk mixture and salt. Mix the ingredients together at low speed for about 1 minute, until they are fully combined. Leave the buttercream uncolored for now and set it aside.

ASSEMBLE THE CAKE

1. Level the cooled cake layers to your desired height (page 31). Fill and stack the cake layers (page 32) with Creamy Coffee Buttercream, then crumb coat the cake (page 37) with Creamy Coffee Buttercream. Chill the crumb-coated cake in the refrigerator for at least 30 minutes.

2. Frost a smooth buttercream finish (page 61) with Creamy Coffee Buttercream. Add the crushed cookies around the bottom of the cake. Refrigerate it while you make the White Chocolate Ganache Drip (page 136).

3. When the White Chocolate Ganache Drip has cooled to drip consistency, add a half drip (page 100) around half of the top of the cake. Chill the cake back in the refrigerator for 5 minutes to let the ganache set.

4. Create the buttercream color palette: Divide the remaining Creamy Coffee Buttercream among four separate bowls. To the first bowl, add 2 drops of AmeriColor Orange and 1 drop of AmeriColor Chocolate Brown to create a burnt orange color. To the second bowl, add 2 drops of AmeriColor Wedgewood to create a muted pastel blue. To the third bowl, add 1 drop of AmeriColor Chocolate Brown to create a light shade of brown. To the fourth bowl, add 5 drops of AmeriColor Chocolate Brown to create a dark brown color.

5. Fit two piping bags with Wilton tip 4B, one piping bag with a Wilton tip 6B and one piping bag with a Wilton tip 2. Transfer the burnt orange buttercream to the piping bag fitted with tip 6B. Transfer the dark brown buttercream to the bag fitted with tip 2. Transfer the remaining two colors to the two piping bags fitted with tip 4B.

6. Create the piped pumpkin crescent: Hover the piping bag fitted with tip 6B about ¼ inch (6 mm) from the surface of the cake and squeeze the bag until the buttercream makes contact with the cake, then slowly pull the bag upward to create a pumpkin shape (A). Continue to pipe pumpkins with tip 6B, spacing them 1 to 2 inches (2.5 to 5 cm) apart in a crescent shape (B). The ends of the crescent should be aligned with the edges of the ganache half drip.

7. Repeat step 6 using the remaining piping bags fitted with a Wilton tip 4B to create smaller pumpkins, filling in all the empty spaces of the crescent shape (C).

8. Use the piping bag fitted with a Wilton tip 2 to pipe a stem on top of each pumpkin (D).

Salted Caramel Chocolate Cake

Yield: 1 triple-layer 6-inch (15-cm) cake or 1 double-layer 8-inch (20-cm) cake
Prep time: 45 minutes   **Bake time:** 32–36 minutes

There are few flavor pairings more decadent than chocolate and caramel. I've been a huge fan ever since I discovered Cadbury Caramello bars as a kid, and this cake is inspired by that nostalgic flavor combination. It features layers of moist chocolate cake, Salted Caramel Buttercream and the easiest homemade salted caramel sauce you'll ever make—no candy thermometer necessary! While all of the components of this cake are easy to make, the most challenging part is creating the decorative salted caramel drip. For best results with the drip, use a piping bag instead of a spoon and take a look at the note following this recipe to ensure your caramel's consistency is perfect for dripping. These two tips should ensure your finished cake looks as beautiful as it tastes.

CHOCOLATE CAKE

2 cups (266 g) all-purpose flour

1⅔ cups (332 g) granulated sugar

⅔ cup (60 g) natural unsweetened cocoa powder

2 tsp (10 g) baking soda

1 tsp baking powder

½ tsp salt

½ cup (120 ml) vegetable oil

2 large eggs, at room temperature

1½ tsp (8 ml) pure vanilla extract

1 cup (240 ml) full-fat buttermilk, at room temperature

1 cup (240 ml) hot coffee or hot water

SALTED CARAMEL

1 batch Salted Caramel (page 139)

MAKE THE CHOCOLATE CAKE

1. Preheat the oven to 350°F (177°C). Prepare three 6-inch (15-cm) or two 8-inch (20-cm) round cake pans by spraying the sides with baking spray and fitting a parchment paper circle to the bottom of each pan.

2. In the bowl of a stand mixer fitted with the paddle attachment, combine the flour, granulated sugar, cocoa powder, baking soda, baking powder and salt. Mix the ingredients together at low speed for 30 seconds to fully combine them. Add the oil, eggs, vanilla and buttermilk and mix the ingredients at low speed until they are just combined. With the mixer still running at low speed, add the hot coffee or water in a slow stream, then increase the mixer's speed to medium and beat the ingredients for about 2 minutes, until the mixture is smooth. The batter will be very thin.

3. Divide the batter evenly between the prepared cake pans. Bake the cakes for 32 to 36 minutes, until a toothpick inserted into the centers comes out clean. Let the cakes cool in their pans for 5 minutes, then remove the cakes from the pans and allow them to cool completely on a wire rack.

MAKE THE SALTED CARAMEL

1. Make 1 batch of Salted Caramel (page 139). Set the Salted Caramel aside.

(continued)

SALTED CARAMEL BUTTERCREAM

1½ cups (339 g) unsalted butter, at room temperature

5¼ cups (630 g) powdered sugar

2 tbsp (30 ml) whole milk, at room temperature

1 tbsp (15 ml) pure vanilla extract

¾ cup (180 ml) Salted Caramel, at room temperature

½ tsp salt

TOPPING

Salted caramel truffles, as needed

NOTE

During step 3, if the Salted Caramel seems too thick for dripping at this point, whisk in some room-temperature heavy cream, ¼ to ½ teaspoon at a time. Continue the process of heating the caramel in the microwave and adding more cream if needed until the consistency is suitable for dripping.

MAKE THE SALTED CARAMEL BUTTERCREAM

1. In the bowl of a stand mixer fitted with the paddle attachment, beat the butter at high speed for 5 to 6 minutes, scraping the bowl and paddle occasionally, until it is fluffy and light. Decrease the mixer's speed to low and add the powdered sugar 2 cups (240 g) at a time, scraping the bowl and paddle after each addition.

2. With the mixer still running at low speed, add the milk, vanilla, Salted Caramel and salt. Mix the ingredients for 1 to 2 minutes, until they are well combined.

ASSEMBLE THE CAKE

1. Level the cooled cake layers to your desired height (page 31). Fill and stack the cake layers (page 32) with Salted Caramel Buttercream, then crumb coat the cake (page 37) with Salted Caramel Buttercream. Chill the crumb-coated cake in the refrigerator for at least 30 minutes to allow the frosting to firm up.

2. Reserve about 1 cup (215 g) of the Salted Caramel Buttercream for the crescent border, then create a semi-naked finish (page 65) with the remaining Salted Caramel Buttercream.

3. Warm the remaining Salted Caramel in the microwave in 10-second spurts, stirring after each one, until the caramel reaches drip consistency (i.e., slightly above room temperature; see Note). Transfer the Salted Caramel to a piping bag. Use clean scissors to cut off a ¼-inch (6 mm) opening at the end of the piping bag. Create a decorative half drip (page 100) around the top edges of the cake with the Salted Caramel.

4. Refrigerate the caramel-dripped cake for 5 to 10 minutes while you fit one piping bag with a Wilton tip 4B and one piping bag with a Wilton tip 1M. Divide the remaining Salted Caramel Buttercream between the two piping bags, then top the cake with a crescent border (page 116) of rosettes and stars. Garnish the cake with the salted caramel truffles.

Tiramisu Layer Cake

Yield: 1 triple-layer 6-inch (15-cm) cake or 1 double-layer 8-inch (20-cm) cake
Prep time: 1 hour 5 minutes   **Bake time:** 30–35 minutes

My husband rarely drinks coffee, yet somehow he naturally gravitates toward tiramisu (it could be because he's Italian). The traditional form is made of ladyfingers that have been soaked in an espresso-liqueur mixture and are then layered with mascarpone cream and dusted with cocoa powder. In this layer-cake version, my Favorite Vanilla Cake (page 126) is a stand-in for the ladyfingers, and it's soaked with espresso (add some liqueur if you prefer), layered with a mascarpone filling, topped with Vanilla-Espresso Buttercream and dusted with cocoa powder. It's the ultimate dessert, perfect for any coffee lover or tiramisu fan.

CAKE

1 batch Favorite Vanilla Cake (page 126)

COFFEE SOAK

½ cup (120 ml) espresso or strong coffee, cold

2 tbsp (30 ml) Amaretto or coffee liqueur (optional)

MASCARPONE FILLING

¾ cup (170 g) unsalted butter, at room temperature

1 cup (226 g) mascarpone cheese, at room temperature

2 cups (240 g) powdered sugar

1 tsp pure vanilla extract

VANILLA-ESPRESSO BUTTERCREAM

1 cup (226 g) unsalted butter, at room temperature

3½ cups (420 g) powdered sugar

2 tsp (10 ml) pure vanilla extract

1½ tbsp (23 ml) whole milk, at room temperature

¼ tsp salt

1½ tsp (2 g) espresso powder

MAKE THE FAVORITE VANILLA CAKE

1. Make 1 batch of the Favorite Vanilla Cake (page 126). Allow the cakes to cool completely before continuing with this recipe; however, do not level them yet.

MAKE THE COFFEE SOAK

1. In a small bowl, combine the espresso and Amaretto (if using).

MAKE THE MASCARPONE FILLING

1. In the bowl of a stand mixer fitted with the paddle attachment, beat the butter and mascarpone cheese at medium-high speed for about 2 minutes, until the mixture is light and fluffy.

2. Decrease the mixer's speed to low, and then add the powdered sugar 1 cup (120 g) at a time, scraping the bowl and paddle as needed. Add the vanilla, then increase the mixer's speed to medium-high and beat the mixture for 3 minutes. Do not overmix the filling.

MAKE THE VANILLA-ESPRESSO BUTTERCREAM

1. In the bowl of a stand mixer fitted with the paddle attachment, beat the butter at high speed for about 5 minutes, until it is light and creamy.

2. Decrease the mixer's speed to low and add the powdered sugar 2 cups (240 g) at a time, scraping the bowl and paddle as needed. Add the vanilla, milk and salt and mix at low speed until the ingredients are fully combined and the frosting is smooth. Mix in the espresso powder.

(continued)

TOPPING

Natural unsweetened cocoa powder, as needed

ASSEMBLE THE CAKE

1. Level the cooled cake layers to your desired height (page 31). Spoon about 3 tablespoons (45 ml) of the Coffee Soak over the surface of the first layer, then place half of the Mascarpone Filling on top of the soaked cake layer and smooth the filling. Place the next cake layer on top and repeat the process of soaking and filling before adding the final cake layer on top, upside down. Add the remaining coffee soak to the top layer of the cake.

2. Crumb coat the cake (page 37) with Vanilla-Espresso Buttercream. Chill the crumb-coated cake in the refrigerator for at least 30 minutes to allow the frosting to firm up. Then use the tutorial on page 66 to frost a semi-naked finish. Chill the frosted cake in the refrigerator for 20 minutes.

3. Fit a piping bag with a Wilton tip 4B, then fill the piping bag with the remaining Vanilla-Espresso Buttercream. Pipe a rope border (page 116) around the top edge of the cake. Using a flour duster or fine-mesh sieve, dust the top of the cake with the cocoa powder.

Chapter 6
RESOURCES

By now, you've probably realized that cake-making is a process that requires a fair amount of planning. There are many times that you'll find yourself planning a trip to the grocery store to get ingredients or calculating how far in advance you can make your cake so that it's ready in time—and still fresh—for an event. You might find yourself Googling ingredient substitutes at the last minute because you don't have time to go to the store.

To save you from stressing out over any part of the process, this chapter answers all the logistical questions you might have: how to make your cake ahead of time, what to do if you can't find cake flour, how to alter a cake recipe for a different pan size and much more. You'll find charts and timelines to set you at ease, plus some bonus content to help you along the way. When you feel prepared and organized going into the cake-making process, there's more room for joy—which, in my opinion, is the most important part of it all.

MAKING & STORING CAKES AHEAD OF TIME

You know those baking competition shows where the contestants get only a few hours to make a showstopper cake? Although these bakers prove to us that it's possible to bake and decorate a majestic cake in a very short amount of time, the process is not without a high level of anxiety (and often a few tears as well). Instead, imagine having all of your elements—beautifully baked cake layers, silky smooth buttercream, all the fillings and decorations you'll be using—made ahead of time and ready to go when it's time to decorate. Sounds like all you're missing is some great background music! Here's how to make and store common cake elements ahead of time.

CAKE LAYERS

After baking the cake layers, wait until they're completely cool to the touch before wrapping them in plastic wrap and storing them at room temperature for up to 2 days.

Alternatively, you can store cake layers in the freezer for up to 2 months. To ensure that they stay extra fresh, I like to wrap the cake layers in one layer of plastic wrap, then one layer of aluminum foil. Then I place them in a ziplock bag (or other freezer-safe airtight container). When you're ready to use the cake layers, keep them wrapped in the aluminum foil and plastic wrap while they thaw at room temperature for at least 2 hours. The excess condensation will escape and gather on top of the foil, which acts as a barrier to keep the cake beneath it from getting soggy.

BUTTERCREAM FROSTING

Place buttercream in an airtight container and store it in the refrigerator for up to 2 weeks. When you're ready to use it, bring it back to room temperature by letting it rest on the counter for 1 to 2 hours. Once the buttercream reaches room temperature, transfer it to the bowl of a stand mixer fitted with the paddle attachment and mix it at low speed for about 1 minute. This will bring the frosting right back to a silky smooth consistency.

You can also store buttercream frosting in the freezer for up to 3 months. To prepare buttercream for the freezer, roll it up in plastic wrap like a burrito, then place it in a ziplock bag or any kind of freezer-safe airtight container. The day before you're ready to use it, place the frozen buttercream in the refrigerator to thaw. Then bring it back to room temperature and remix it in the bowl of a stand mixer at low speed to bring it back to frosting consistency.

CHOCOLATE GANACHE

Place chocolate ganache in an airtight container and store it in the refrigerator for up to 2 weeks. If you'll be using it to drip a cake, gently heat it in the microwave in 10- to 15-second intervals, stirring after each one, until the ganache reaches drip consistency (page 97).

SALTED CARAMEL

Store Salted Caramel (page 139) in an airtight container in the refrigerator for up to 2 weeks. When you're ready to use the Salted Caramel as a drip, heat it in the microwave in 10- to 15-second intervals, stirring after each one, until it reaches drip consistency (page 97). If you're using the Salted Caramel as a filling or drizzle, bring it to room temperature before adding it to the cake with a piping bag.

CRUMB-COATED CAKES

Store crumb-coated cakes in the refrigerator up to 1 day ahead of frosting and decorating. The crumb coat layer of buttercream acts as a barrier that helps keep mois-ture inside, but after a day or so the cake beneath may start to dry out without a thicker layer of buttercream to protect it.

FULLY DECORATED CAKES

The refrigerator is my favorite place to store fully decorated cakes, as I find the cold temperature helps all the decorations set perfectly. Either place the cake in a box or store it on a serving plate uncovered for 2 to 3 days. Since the buttercream frosting helps keep the moisture inside, there's no need to worry about the cake drying out within this time frame. Do keep in mind that any strong-smelling foods inside your refrigerator may get absorbed by the cake. To lessen the chance of this happening, store aromatic foods in airtight containers.

Although I use the refrigerator to store fully decorated cakes 100 percent of the time, you can also store them covered at room temperature for up to 3 days. Before you store a cake at room temperature, make sure that it doesn't have any frostings or fillings that require refrigeration.

> **TIP:**
>
> The term *room temperature* refers to an environment that's ideally between 65 and 68°F (18° and 20°C).

Lastly, you can store a fully decorated cake in the freezer for up to 3 months, if necessary. To do so, place the cake in the freezer for 4 hours to let everything solidify, then wrap the cake in a layer of plastic wrap and a layer of aluminum foil before popping it back into the freezer. To thaw the cake, remove the plastic and aluminum layers and place it in the refrigerator 1 day before you plan on serving it.

CAKE DECORATING TIMELINES

Let's say you're making a cake for an event on a Saturday at 2:00 p.m. Let's also say you have a full-time day job and a few kids at home, so you can work on the cake only after 8:00 p.m. Oh, and I forgot to mention you're busy on Friday night. How far in advance can you make the cake and keep it fresh for the event?

Following are some sample timelines to help you plan your workflow. When reading these timelines, keep in mind that you can do as much or as little as you'd like on the day the cake is due. The closer you can bake and decorate the cake to the time it's due, the fresher the cake will be. These examples simply show how far in advance you can begin the process while keeping the cake fresh.

SEVEN-DAY SAMPLE TIMELINE

Sunday	Monday	Tuesday	Wednesday	Thursday	Friday	Saturday
Bake and freeze cake layers Make frosting	Make chocolate ganache		Thaw cake layers Thaw frosting Build and crumb coat cake	Frost and decorate cake		Cake due

FIVE-DAY SAMPLE TIMELINE

Tuesday	Wednesday	Thursday	Friday	Saturday
Bake and freeze cake layers	Make frosting Make chocolate ganache	Thaw cake layers Thaw frosting Build and crumb coat cake	Frost and decorate cake	Cake due

THREE-DAY SAMPLE TIMELINE

Thursday	Friday	Saturday
Bake cake layers (store at room temperature) Make frosting	Build and crumb coat cake Make chocolate ganache Frost cake	Add ganache drips and other finishing touches Cake due

TWO-DAY SAMPLE TIMELINE

Friday	Saturday
Bake cake layers (store at room temperature) Make frosting Build and crumb coat cake	Make chocolate ganache Frost and decorate cake Cake due

COMMON INGREDIENT SUBSTITUTES

Since I spend so much time writing and testing cake recipes, I know how much thought and energy goes into an ingredients list. This is why I recommend following a recipe exactly when you're making it for the first time. While it may involve making that extra trip to the grocery store, the effort will be worth it, as you'll get to experience the fullness of the recipe, just as it was intended to look and taste. After the first time, though, feel free to experiment with ingredient substitutes, whether you're in a pinch or purely curious about different outcomes! Here are some common substitutes to try.

Specified Ingredient	Substitute
1 cup (120 g) unsifted cake flour	1 cup (123 g) Homemade Cake Flour Recipe (page 216)
1 cup (240 ml) buttermilk	1 cup (240 ml) Homemade Buttermilk Recipe (page 217)
1 cup (240 g) sour cream	1 cup (240 g) full-fat plain yogurt
¼ tsp baking soda	1 tsp baking powder
1 tsp baking powder	½ tsp cream of tartar plus ¼ tsp baking soda
½ cup (45 g) natural unsweetened cocoa powder	½ cup (45 g) Dutch-process cocoa powder (replace the amount of baking soda in the recipe with twice the amount of baking powder)
½ cup (45 g) Dutch-process cocoa powder	½ cup (45 g) natural unsweetened cocoa powder (replace the amount of baking powder in the recipe with half the amount of baking soda)
1 cup (240 ml) heavy cream	1 cup (240 ml) whole milk plus 1 tbsp (15 ml) melted butter
1 cup (200 g) light brown sugar	1 cup (200 g) dark brown sugar or 1 cup (200 g) granulated sugar plus 1 tbsp (15 ml) molasses
1 cup (200 g) dark brown sugar	1 cup (200 g) light brown sugar or 1 cup (200 g) granulated sugar plus 2 tbsp (30 ml) molasses
1 tsp pure vanilla extract	1 tsp vanilla bean paste or ½ tsp vanilla powder or one-third of a vanilla bean, cut open and scraped
1 cup (240 ml) whole milk	1 cup (240 ml) skim or low-fat milk plus 2 tbsp (30 ml) melted butter

Homemade Cake Flour Recipe

There's a reason why the majority of my cake recipes call for cake flour instead of all-purpose or plain flour. The short answer is that using cake flour is one of the keys to making cakes extra light and fluffy! You can find cake flour in the baking aisle of most grocery stores, but if it is something you don't have access to, I have great news: You can easily convert the all-purpose flour you already have in your pantry to homemade cake flour that's just as effective.

A quick word on metric weight: This homemade cake flour weighs more than store-bought cake flour. This is because it's made with all-purpose flour, which is naturally heavier than cake flour. When substituting with homemade cake flour, disregard the original metric measurement for the cake flour in the recipe. Instead of measuring by weight, measure homemade cake flour manually.

---

2 tbsp (16 g) cornstarch

1 cup (133 g) all-purpose flour

1. Place the cornstarch in a 1-cup (240-g) dry measuring cup.

2. Spoon the flour on top of the cornstarch and level it off with the back of a butter knife to measure exactly 1 cup (133 g).

3. Repeat steps 1 and 2 until you have the amount of cake flour the recipe calls for, then sift it all together in a large bowl four to six times. I know, it's a lot of sifting, but it's worth it!

4. Remeasure the cake flour by spooning and leveling it into your measuring cup, then use it in the recipe. Since all the sifting done in step 3 aerates the flour, it tends to increase in volume. This second measurement is necessary to prevent adding more flour than you need, which can result in a dense cake.

You can make large amounts of this cake flour ahead of time and store it in an airtight container in your pantry. This way, you won't have to repeat the measuring-and-sifting process every time you make a cake. This recipe is a little more time-intensive than buying actual cake flour, but it works in a pinch.

Note that you will see some recipes in this book that call for all-purpose flour. I don't recommend substituting cake flour in those recipes, since they probably need more structure than cake flour can provide. That said, you can absolutely use this homemade cake flour recipe any time you're working with a recipe that calls for cake flour and you don't have store-bought cake flour on hand.

Homemade Buttermilk Recipe

I have a confession to make: I almost never have store-bought buttermilk in my refrigerator. Okay, I know it's shocking! But before you start judging my lack of milk variety, allow me to explain: While a few of my recipes call for buttermilk and I do sing the praises of its moisture-making power, it's not something I can justify buying regularly since I never use the whole carton. What I do have in my refrigerator at all times is whole milk. This is partly because I have a toddler at home, partly because most of my cake recipes call for whole milk and partly because you can easily turn whole milk into buttermilk like magic. Here's how to do it:

1 tbsp (15 ml) distilled white vinegar or fresh lemon juice

1 scant cup (225 ml) whole milk (see Note)

Pour the vinegar into a small liquid measuring cup. Add the milk until the liquid level reaches the 1-cup (240-ml) mark. Stir the mixture and let it sit for 10 to 15 minutes, after which you may see a light separation (or curdling) forming between the milk and acid. Allow the buttermilk to come to room temperature before using it in a cake recipe.

NOTE

This recipe works best with whole milk because it has the most fat, which gives your cake the best texture. However, it will work with any kind of milk in a pinch (even dairy-free milks).

CAKE PAN SIZES & SUBSTITUTIONS

Cake recipes are always written for specific pan sizes. You'll find that most of my recipes yield 6 to 7 cups (1.4 to 1.8 L) of batter, enough for three 6-inch (15-cm) layers or two 8-inch (20-cm) layers. In case you don't yet have a certain pan size or need to scale a recipe for any reason, the following table provides some common sizes that you can use as a starting point in your substitution.

A couple of things to keep in mind before substituting cake pans:

The "Total Volume" column refers to the amount a cake pan can hold when filled all the way to the top. Be sure to fill a cake pan no more than two-thirds full to account for rising.

Baking times are approximate. Keep a close eye on the cake when making pan substitutions to check for doneness.

TIP:

To bake any of my cake recipes as cupcakes, fill the cupcake pans' wells no more than two-thirds full and bake the cupcakes at 350°F (177°C) for 15 to 18 minutes. Note that 6 cups (1.4 L) of cake batter will yield 24 cupcakes.

Pan Size	Total Volume	One-Half to Two-Thirds Full	Baking Temperature	Approximate Baking Time
Round Pans				
4 x 2 inches (10 x 5 cm)	1½ cups (360 ml)	¾–1 cup (180–238 ml)	350°F (177°C)	18–24 minutes
6 x 2 inches (15 x 5 cm)	4 cups (960 ml)	2–2⅔ cups (480–638 ml)	350°F (177°C)	30–35 minutes
7 x 2 inches (18 x 5 cm)	5 cups (1.2 L)	2½–3⅓ cups (600–799 ml)	350°F (177°C)	35–40 minutes
8 x 2 inches (20 x 5 cm)	6 cups (1.4 L)	3–4 cups (720–960 ml)	350°F (177°C)	35–40 minutes
9 x 2 inches (23 x 5 cm)	8 cups (1.9 L)	4–5⅓ cups (960 ml to 1.3 L)	350°F (177°C)	40–45 minutes
10 x 2 inches (25 x 5 cm)	11 cups (2.6 L)	5½–7⅓ cups (1.3–1.8 L)	350°F (177°C)	40–45 minutes
12 x 2 inches (30 x 5 cm)	15 cups (3.6 L)	7½–10 cups (1.8–2.4 L)	350°F (177°C)	40–45 minutes
Square Pans				
8 x 2 inches (20 x 5 cm)	8 cups (1.9 L)	4–5⅓ cups (960 ml to 1.3 L)	350°F (177°C)	40–45 minutes
9 x 2 inches (23 x 5 cm)	10 cups (2.4 L)	5–6⅔ cups (1.2–1.6 L)	350°F (177°C)	45–50 minutes
10 x 2 inches (25 x 5 cm)	12 cups (2.9 L)	6–8 cups (1.4–1.9 L)	350°F (177°C)	50–55 minutes
Rectangular Pans				
11 x 7 inches (28 x 18 cm)	10 cups (2.4 L)	5–6⅔ cups (1.2–1.6 L)	350°F (177°C)	45–50 minutes
9 x 13 inches (23 x 33 cm)	15 cups (3.6 L)	7½–10 cups (1.8–2.4 L)	350°F (177°C)	40–45 minutes

WORKING WITH YOUR UNIQUE OVEN

Do you know what kind of oven you have? If not, go take a peek inside. Research the serial number. Really get to know it like a companion. It's going to be a huge part of your cake-making journey, and since baking is such a precise science, you can truly benefit from knowing what you're working with. You may even get better results with your bakes after reading this section.

TYPES OF OVENS

There are two main types of ovens when it comes to home baking: conventional and convection. Conventional ovens have a stationary heat source in the bottom of the appliance that causes heat to rise and radiate throughout. It surrounds your cake layers with heat and helps cook them evenly. Whether gas or electric, conventional ovens are ideal for baking. Unless the oven type is specified, you can assume that any baking recipe is written for a conventional oven.

Convection ovens, also called fan-assisted ovens, have a fan inside that circulates hot air, creating an even temperature throughout the oven. While you can certainly bake cakes in a convection oven, the constant heat circulation tends to bake them faster and at a hotter temperature. If you don't know how to adapt a recipe to suit your convection oven, this can easily lead to burned edges, sunken middles and lopsided bakes.

Some bakers have no problem baking in a fan-assisted oven without making any alterations, but if your cakes have a tendency to bake too quickly, here's how to troubleshoot:

Turn off the fan to transform your convection oven into a conventional oven.

Since convection ovens run hotter than conventional ovens set to the same temperature, you'll need to reduce the temperature indicated in the recipe. Instead of 350°F (177°C), set your convection oven temperature to 325°F (163°C) for best results.

Check your cakes 5 to 10 minutes before the baking time indicated in the recipe.

OVEN TEMPERATURE VARIATION

Here's the thing about ovens: They aren't always accurate. Unless you have a brand-new oven or get your oven calibrated regularly, chances are that your oven may not be the exact temperature you set it to. It could be off by a few degrees or fifty . . . or more! The only true way to tell is by placing an oven thermometer inside. These inexpensive little gadgets are meant to live inside your oven, always giving you an accurate reading of the temperature you're truly baking at.

An oven that's too hot will bake your cake too quickly, and an oven that's too cold will take forever to bake your cake through. Once you know the exact internal oven temperature, though, it's easy to adapt by either reducing or increasing the oven temperature you set.

For example: If the recipe calls for preheating the oven to 350°F (177°C), but the internal oven thermometer is reading 300°F (149°C), try setting the oven to 400°F (200°C) instead. Keep checking the internal oven thermometer and making changes until it reaches the temperature you need.

ACKNOWLEDGMENTS

To the readers and supporters of Sugar & Sparrow: Thank you. It is seeing you thrive in your cake-making and hearing your success stories that keeps the wind in my sails. You've inspired the content in this book more than you know.

To my husband, Josiah: You are the best partner I could have ever asked for. This book would never have happened had you not encouraged me to start a blog and fully supported me every single step of the way. Thank you for taking a thousand photos of my hands holding cakes and whisks and frosting-covered paddles up in the air, for lending countless hours of design and creativity to Sugar & Sparrow, for being an idea machine and constant source of inspiration and for sampling far more cakes than you signed up for. I think you're brilliant, and this book is exactly what I envisioned because of you.

To my son, Theo: You probably won't remember all the time you spent with me in the kitchen, but I will never forget it. We made some sweet memories whipping up recipes for this book. You may have always left the kitchen looking like it was hit by a tornado, but I wouldn't have wanted to test these recipes any other way. You're my dream sous-chef.

To my friends near and far who taste-tested these recipes, baked them in their own ovens, let me question them intensely about things like spice level and moisture and fluffiness, helped me choose between photos, weighed in on the cover design, checked in on me and cheered me on endlessly: Lauren, Mel, Heather, Meghan, Jacey, Sophie and Jael, Brianna and Hendrix, Peter and Toni, Matt and Erin and Rachael, thank you for being guiding lights on this journey and making me feel so upheld.

To Sarah, Vanessa and Rups: Thank you for sincerely testing my recipes, listening to my cake epiphanies and nerding out with me over what makes the perfect cake layer. You have helped grow my confidence as a baker, and I am forever thankful to have friends whom I could trust to bounce these recipe ideas off of.

To Abi: Thank you for contributing your incredible photography skills to this book, making photo shoots so much fun and creating photos that I'll cherish forever. So many of these are going in frames.

To Micah: Thank you for following me around the kitchen with your camera for way longer than you anticipated, all so we could film an epic promo video for this book. You went the extra mile, and it means the world to me.

To Kendyl and Taylor: Thank you for being the best nannies in the world and caring for Theo, so that I could have a few solo hours of baking and writing every week. I would not have made my deadlines without your help and genuine love for my boy.

To my amazing editors, Ari and Sarah: I felt your support the whole way through. Thank you both for being so collaborative, communicative, detail-oriented and for helping shape this book into something I am incredibly proud of. You went above and beyond to test cake recipes, compare them and even consult your friends to help choose the very best for this book. I could not be happier that we were teamed up for this project.

To the entire Page Street Publishing team: Thank you for choosing me and believing that I had a story to tell. I couldn't have asked for a more supportive team behind this book. You made this whole process an absolute dream come true.

To all the bakers, bloggers and authors in this wonderful online community I have found myself a part of: Thank you. You constantly inspire me, challenge me to try new things and keep the fire for caking alive. I hope this book brings you much joy as you learn, grow and bake along!

ABOUT THE AUTHOR

Whitney DePaoli is the writer, photographer and cake artist behind Sugar & Sparrow, a popular baking blog that focuses on approachable cake recipes and tutorials for people of all skill levels.

Whitney's fascination with baking began at a young age, inspired by her mother's lemon squares and casserole-dish sheet cakes. Self-taught every step of the way, Whitney's curiosity in the kitchen led her to a passion for cake decorating, and she went on to spend many years running a custom cake business.

She now spends her time teaching others the things she continues to learn via her website, social channels and online Cake Basics video series. Her recipes and photography have been featured in countless web and print publications, including Food Network, Buzz-Feed's Tasty, Wilton, feedfeed and *American Cake Decorating* magazine.

Whitney lives in the Pacific Northwest with her husband, son and a pantry full of cake ingredients. *Anyone Can Cake* is her first book. Find Whitney at sugarandsparrow.com, or follow along on social media for more recipes, tutorials and tasty cake pictures.

@sugarandsparrowco

youtube.com/sugarandsparrow

@sugarandsparrow

INDEX